英汉对照管理丛书 ⑤

做个学习者

LEARNER's Pocketbook

【英】保罗·海登 著
（Paul Hayden）

菲尔·黑尔斯顿（Phil Hailstone） 绘图

王 薇 译

U0653816

上海交通大学 出版社
SHANGHAI JIAO TONG UNIVERSITY PRESS

内容提要

本书为"英汉对照管理丛书"之一，主要介绍了如何提高自己的学习力，如：如何集中精力，如何创造时间，学习的四个阶段，什么是学习曲线，如何制定学习计划，各种记忆技巧，你会遇到哪些学习障碍等内容。

本书为英汉对照，读者可以在学习知识的时候学到地道的英文表达。

© Paul Hayden 2005

This translation of Strategy Pocketbook first published in 2015 is published by arrangement with Management Pocketbooks Limited

版权合同登记号：图字：09-2013-720 号

图书在版编目（CIP）数据

做个学习者 /（英）海登（Hayden, P.）著；王薇译.
—上海：上海交通大学出版社，2015
（英汉对照管理丛书）
ISBN 978-7-313-12551-4

Ⅰ．做... Ⅱ．①海... ②王... Ⅲ．企业管理－英、汉
Ⅳ．F270

中国版本图书馆 CIP 数据核字（2015）第 014698 号

做个学习者

著　　者：[英] 保罗·海登　　　　　译　　者：王　薇
出版发行：上海交通大学出版社　　地　　址：上海市番禺路 951 号
邮政编码：200030　　　　　　　　电　　话：021-64071208
出 版 人：韩建民
印　　制：常熟市文化印刷有限公司　经　　销：全国新华书店
开　　本：880mm×1230mm 1/32　印　　张：8
字　　数：199 千字
版　　次：2015 年 1 月第 1 版　　　印　　次：2015 年 1 月第 1 次印刷
书　　号：ISBN 978-7-313-12551-4/F
定　　价：28.00 元

编辑的话

嗨，大家好！

最早出版这个系列的书（英汉对照管理袖珍手册）是在 2002 年，随后我们又在 2004 年和 2007 年分别推出了第二辑和第三辑。这套丛书（共 50 本）被很多 500 强企业用作培训教材，也被很多读者整套收藏。

这一次，我们对书的开本做了调整。我们给您留出了做笔记的空间。您可以把您查阅的英文单词、词组和句式写在原文下面空白的 Notes 处，也可以把您阅读过程中的所思所想写在此处，把这本书真正变成属于您自己的书。

另外，我们对中文字体也作了调整，让您阅读起来更为轻松。

因为这些调整，书不再那么袖珍，所以丛书名也改为了"英汉对照管理丛书"。

如果您有什么建议和反馈，请别忘了告诉我们！（请发邮件至：wangliatcn@qq.com）

再一次，祝您阅读愉快！

汪 俪

2014 年 12 月

目　录

CONTENTS

Global business leaders are crying out for more brainpower, the development of **intellectual capital**, and investment in the most powerful currency in the world – the currency of **intelligence**.

This growing development of the awareness *by* intelligence *of* intelligence and the fact that this quality is not only multiple but can be nurtured and grown, is one of the great beacons of hope for the future of our race. When humankind becomes truly mentally literate – understanding both the alphabet of the neurophysiology of the brain and the alphabet of its behaviour, including memory, creativity, thinking, reading and learning – the world will, in all probability, approach the utopia which for many millennia has been the dream of so many different societies.

Paul Hayden's delightful **The Learner's Pocketbook** is a considered and intelligent introduction to this intriguing field, and will start the 'learner of learning' off in the right direction – on a journey that will provide immeasurable satisfactions and reward.

Tony Buzan

　　全球商业领袖们都求贤若渴，希望发展**智力资本**，投资世界上最坚挺的货币——**智力**货币。

　　人们逐渐意识到智力的重要性，以及智力不仅是多种多样的，而且是可以后天培养的，这一事实点亮了人类未来希望的灯塔。当人类真正通晓了大脑的活动，也就是理解了大脑神经生理学的字母表以及它的行为的字母表，包括记忆、创造力、思考、阅读和学习，世界将很可能进入乌托邦社会，而这正是几千年来不同社会人们的愿望。

　　保罗·海登的**《做个学习者》**是作者深思熟虑的思想智慧果实，吸引我们进入这个有趣的领域。这本书将引领那些正在学习如何学习的学习者走上正确的道路。在学习旅程中，他们将收获巨大的满足和回报。

——托尼·布赞

HOW TO USE THIS BOOK

FIRST STEPS

1. List key words/headings of your existing knowledge of how to learn, write down the questions you want this book to answer and the **benefits to you** of learning how to learn.

2. Browse **quickly** through the book looking at contents, pictures, diagrams, headings, subjects. If it will **not** answer your questions or give you the benefits you seek: **DO NOT READ IT**. If it **will**:

- Ensure you are in the right physical and emotional state for learning
- Browse more slowly, taking in also the book's organisation and structure
- When ready to read in detail, choose your environment carefully, take regular breaks
- As you read, mark pages, make notes, colour in diagrams, complete the exercises
- Skip tricky text and refer back to it later
- Use what you are learning, practise and get actively involved
- When you have finished reading, summarise key points. Apply what you have learned – otherwise you have not learned

We remember: 20% of what we read, 30% of what we hear, 40% of what we see, 50% of what we say, 60% of what we do, **90% of what we read, hear, see, say and do**

So do more than just read this book! Celebrate your success and continue to learn.

Notes

_____

_____

_____

_____

_____

如何使用本书

第一步

1. 列出你已经掌握的有关如何学习知识的关键词、关键标题，写下你希望本书能回答的问题，以及学会如何学习的**好处**。

2. **快速**浏览本书，留意目录、图表、标题和主题。如果它回答**不了**你的问题或者无法给你想要的益处，**就不要读下去了**。反之，如果它**能**的话：

- 确保你处在良好的身心状态下以保障学习的效率
- 慢点浏览，注意本书的组织和结构
- 打算仔细阅读时，选择良好的学习环境，保证正常的休息
- 阅读时，标记页数，做笔记，在图表里用彩色标注，完成练习
- 跳过难读的内容，之后再回过头阅读
- 使用所学的内容，多练习，积极参与
- 读完后，总结关键点。运用所学内容，否则的话，学习就没有效果

我们能记住阅读内容的 20%，听到内容的 30%，看到内容的 40%，说过内容的 50%，做过事情的 60%，**既看过、听过、见过，也说过、做过的事情的 90%。**

多做点事情，不要光读这本书。庆祝自己的成功，再接再厉。

BRAIN POWER
脑 力

BRAIN POWER

VITAL STATISTICS

- Average adult brain weighs 3 lbs (1.4 kg) = 1 1/2 bags of sugar

- The brain is 70% water

- The brain uses 25% of the body's oxygen and blood supply, but is only 3% of bodyweight

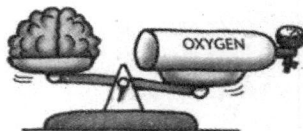

The brain is a muscle. The more you use it, the stronger and bigger it gets. Researchers at the Institute of Neurology at University College London scanned the brains of 16 London cab drivers. They discovered that the part of the brain that stores the mental maps of the capital had grown in size. The longer the cabbie had been driving, the bigger the increase in brain size.

Notes

脑力

重要数据

- 普通成年人大脑重 3 磅（1.4 千克），相当于 1.5 袋糖的重量。

- 大脑成分的 70% 是水。

- 大脑占用了身体 25% 的氧气和血液供应，却只有人体体重的 3%。

大脑是肌肉。使用得越多，它就越强大。伦敦大学学院神经病学研究所的研究员们对 16 名伦敦出租车司机进行了大脑扫描。他们发现，司机大脑中存储伦敦地图的部分有所增大。司机开车的时间越长，增长就越大。

BRAIN POWER

NEURONS

- The brain has 10–15 billion neurons (over twice the number of people in the world)

- It is not the number of neurons that determines intelligence but the number of **connections**

- There are at least 10 trillion (10,000,000,000,000) connections, called synapses

- A synapse is the point where the axon of one neuron connects with the dendrite of another

20,000
neurons would fit on a pin head

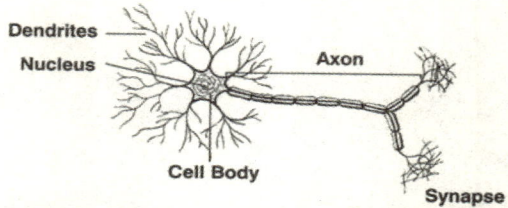

Notes

_____

_____

_____

_____

_____

神经元

- 大脑有100亿～150亿个神经元(是世界上人口数量的两倍多)。

- 决定智力的不是神经元的数量，而是**连结**的数量。

- 人脑中至少有10万亿个连结，被称作**突触**。

- 突触是一个神经元的轴突与另一个神经元的树突的连接点。

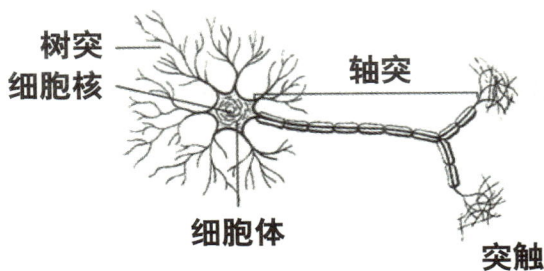

一个大头针的
针头可以容纳
2万个神经元。

BRAIN POWER

BRAIN WAVES

In 1929 German psychiatrist Hans Verger recorded electrical activity in the human brain. He became the *laughing stock* of the scientific world. Only three years later Edgar Adrian won a Nobel prize for demonstrating the electrical activity in the brain. We now know there are four electrical brain waves. Each oscillates at a different number of cycles per second.

Alpha Waves (Oscillating at a rate of 8–12 cycles per second)
Emitted when we are in a relaxed, meditative state, which facilitates inspiration, fast assimilation of facts and heightened memory. The ideal state for learning.

Beta Waves (Oscillating at 18–40 cycles per second)
Emitted when we are wide awake, active and figuring out complex problems.

Theta Waves (Oscillating at 4–7 cycles per second)
Emitted when we are in a state of high mental creativity – daydreaming, and the early stages of sleep, when we dream. When flashes of inspiration can occur.

Delta Waves (Oscillating at 0.5–3 cycles per second)
Emitted when we are in deep dreamless sleep or unconscious.

More than one brain wave can be emitted at any one time. One type will dominate, which describes the *brain state* you are in.

Notes

脑力

脑电波

1929 年，德国精神病学家汉斯·贝格尔记录了人脑中的脑电活动，他因此成了科学界的**笑柄**。仅仅 3 年后，埃德加·阿德里安却因为演示大脑中的脑电活动而获得了诺贝尔奖。现在我们知道共有 4 种脑电波。每种脑电波每秒振动的次数都不同。

α 波（每秒振动 8 ~ 12 次）
当人处于放松、沉思的状态时，大脑会产生 α 波。它会增强灵感，加速记忆。这是学习的最佳状态。

β 波（每秒振动 18 ~ 40 次）
当我们高度清醒、兴奋、思考复杂问题时，大脑会产生 β 波。

θ 波（每秒振动 4 ~ 7 次）
当大脑处于高度精神创造状态时，就会产生 θ 波，如白日梦，及刚开始入眠做梦时，会产生阵阵灵感。

δ 波（每秒振动 0.5 ~ 3 次）
当我们沉睡无梦或是无意识时，大脑会产生 δ 波。

任何时候大脑都会发射不止一种脑电波。其中会有一种占主导地位，它也就决定了你处于哪一种大脑状态。

BRAIN POWER

THREE BRAINS

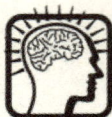

Neocortex
(cortex) ▶ **Intellectual brain**

Comprises 2-sided cerebrum, left and right brain
Makes up 80% of the brain's mass
Back processes visual data, the side processes auditory
data and the centre strip processes data from touch
Controls intellectual processes – talking, seeing,
hearing, reasoning, thinking, problem solving

Mammalian brain
(limbic system) ▶ **Emotional brain**

Contains hypothalamus, pituitary gland and hippo campus
Plays a vital role in long-term memory
Controls emotion, sexuality, health, immune system, sleep

Reptilian brain
(brain stem) ▶ **Instinctive brain**

Stems from the spinal column
Controls basic instincts – breathing, heart rate, sense of
territory, flight or fight brain

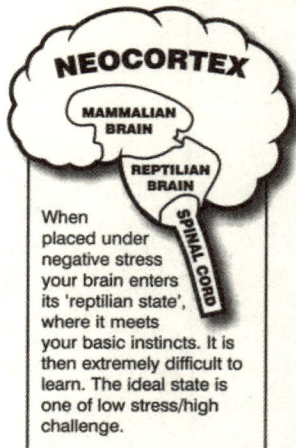

NEOCORTEX

MAMMALIAN BRAIN

REPTILIAN BRAIN

SPINAL CORD

When placed under negative stress your brain enters its 'reptilian state', where it meets your basic instincts. It is then extremely difficult to learn. The ideal state is one of low stress/high challenge.

Notes

_____

_____

_____

_____

_____

三个大脑

新皮层
（大脑皮层） ▶ **智能大脑**

包括左右两个脑半球。

占大脑重量的 80%。

后部处理视觉数据，边缘处理听觉数据，

中间地带处理触觉数据。

控制智力过程，如说、看、听、推理、思考、

解决问题。

哺乳类脑
（边缘系统） ▶ **情感大脑**

包括下丘脑、垂体腺和海马体。

对长期记忆起至关重要的作用。

控制情感、性欲、健康、免疫系统和睡眠。

爬虫类脑
（脑干） ▶ **本能大脑**

连接脊柱。

控制基本本能——呼吸、心跳、领域意识、战斗或逃跑反应。

新皮层

哺乳类脑

爬虫类脑

脊髓

在消极性压力下，你的大脑会处于"爬虫状态"，使你的基本本能得到满足。在这种状态下学习会很难。理想状态是低压力／高挑战。

BRAIN POWER

LEFT & RIGHT BRAIN

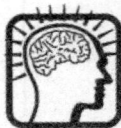

L ogical brain

a **R** tistic brain

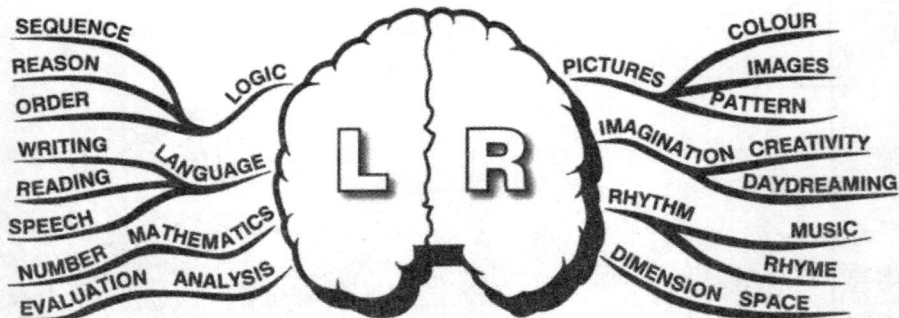

Left brain: SEQUENCE, REASON, ORDER, LOGIC, WRITING, READING, SPEECH, LANGUAGE, NUMBER, MATHEMATICS, EVALUATION, ANALYSIS

Right brain: COLOUR, IMAGES, PATTERN, PICTURES, IMAGINATION, CREATIVITY, DAYDREAMING, RHYTHM, MUSIC, RHYME, DIMENSION, SPACE

Notes

_____

_____

_____

_____

_____

脑力

左右脑

逻辑大脑（左脑）　　　　　　　　艺术大脑（右脑）

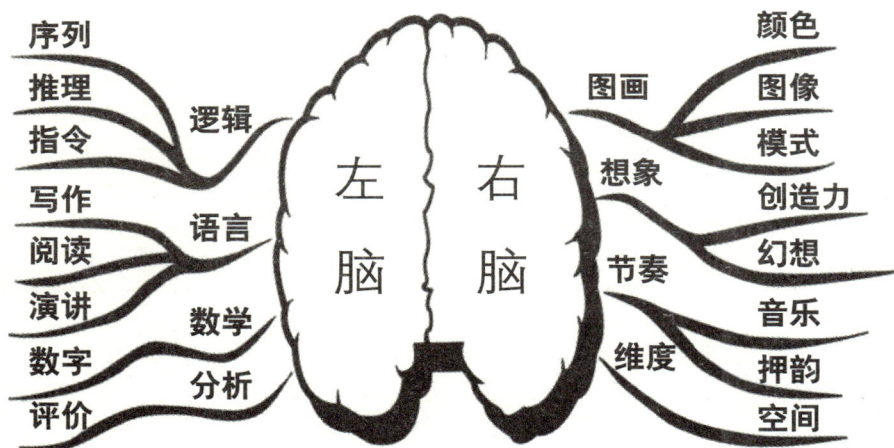

序列
推理
指令　　　逻辑
写作
阅读　　　语言
演讲
数字　　　数学
评价　　　分析

左脑　右脑

图画　　颜色
　　　　图像
想象　　模式
　　　　创造力
节奏　　幻想
　　　　音乐
维度　　押韵
　　　　空间

BRAIN POWER

LEFT & RIGHT BRAIN

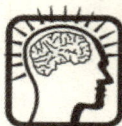

In more recent years neuroscientists have argued that the view that the left and right hemispheres carry out different functions is too simplistic. This *lateralisation theory* is now out of date.

They favour the view that the brain carries out a wide range of functions, the precise centres of which are not yet fully mapped. Some that have been identified are:

- *Wernicke's area* – manages the comprehension of the spoken language

- *Broca's area* – manages muscle control of the throat and mouth used in the spoken word

- *Somosensory area* – receives and processes taste, plus the messages and sensations from your skin

Notes

脑力

左右脑

近几年，神经系统科学家们认为左右脑有不同功能的观点过于简单。这种**偏侧性理论**现在已经过时了。

他们支持大脑有广泛功能的观点。大脑的精确中心还没有完全被确定。已经确定的中心有：

· **威尼克区**——负责口头语言的理解

· **布若卡氏区**——负责说话时喉咙和嘴巴的肌肉控制

· **躯体感觉中枢**——接受并处理味觉以及皮肤的信息、感觉

BRAIN POWER

LEFT & RIGHT BRAIN

Further research by Ned Hermann in the 1980s identified *laterality* of the limbic system. Subsequent work has developed and proven brain quadrants, as illustrated in this simplistic diagram:

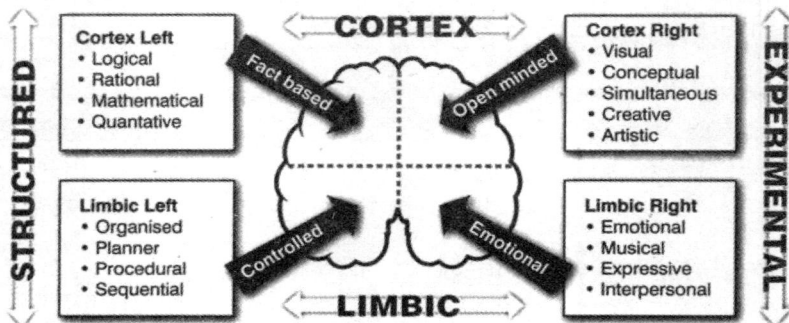

STRUCTURED

CORTEX

Cortex Left
- Logical
- Rational
- Mathematical
- Quantative

Fact based

Open minded

Cortex Right
- Visual
- Conceptual
- Simultaneous
- Creative
- Artistic

EXPERIMENTAL

Limbic Left
- Organised
- Planner
- Procedural
- Sequential

Controlled

Emotional

Limbic Right
- Emotional
- Musical
- Expressive
- Interpersonal

LIMBIC

Notes

脑力

左右脑

　　20 世纪 80 年代，内德·赫尔曼做了关于脑边缘系统**偏侧性**的进一步研究。他提出并证明了脑象限。请看下面的简单图解。

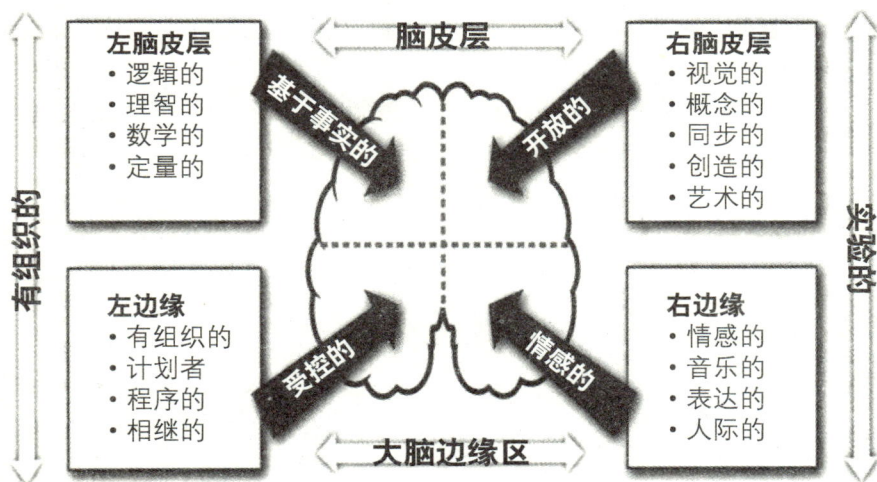

脑皮层

左脑皮层
· 逻辑的
· 理智的
· 数学的
· 定量的

基于事实的

开放的

右脑皮层
· 视觉的
· 概念的
· 同步的
· 创造的
· 艺术的

有组织的

实验的

左边缘
· 有组织的
· 计划者
· 程序的
· 相继的

受控的

情感的

右边缘
· 情感的
· 音乐的
· 表达的
· 人际的

大脑边缘区

BRAIN POWER

LEFT & RIGHT BRAIN

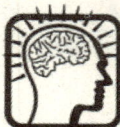

Even though left and right brain theory has been enhanced, it is still true that combining the **L**eft and **R**ight brain will increase your **L**ea**R**ning

For example:

Learning a song:	Learning with mind maps:
• Left brain processes the words	• Left brain processes words and order
• Right brain processes the music	• Right brain processes colour and images
Combine both by singing	**Combine both in a mind map**

Notes

_____

_____

_____

_____

_____

脑力

左右脑

尽管左右脑理论得到了改进，但左右脑合作能加速学习却是肯定的。

例如：

学习唱歌	思维导图助学习
• 左脑处理歌词	• 左脑处理单词和顺序
• 右脑处理音乐	• 右脑处理颜色和图像
两者结合来唱歌	两者结合于思维导图

BRAIN POWER

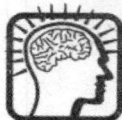

MALE & FEMALE BRAIN

Brain scans have been able to identify differences in male and female brains. The degree to which your brain conforms to the male/female pattern is determined by the level of testosterone your brain received as a foetus.

The female brain has:

- A larger Corpus Callosum, the link between the left and the right brain
- Lower level of testosterone – more likely to be compliant and co-operative
- Higher levels of dopamine – responsible for alerting the brain to information and maintaining attention. The female brain needs less stimulus to maintain attention
- Higher levels of serotonin – responsible for engaging the emotional area of the brain. The female brain is less likely to override its emotional responses
- A greater capacity for linguistic processing

Generally, females should:

- Use both hemispheres of the brain simultaneously
- Multi-task their learning, ie learn several things, or use several learning methods at once
- Use their linguistic strength in learning
- Consider a learning set

Notes

_____

_____

_____

_____

_____

脑力

男性和女性大脑

通过大脑扫描可以发现男性和女性大脑的区别。你的大脑与男性或女性大脑模式的契合度是由胎儿时期大脑接受的睾丸素程度决定的。

女性大脑有：

• 一个较大的胼胝体，它是左右大脑的连接

• 较低的睾丸素值——更容易顺从、合作

• 较高的多巴胺值——提醒大脑注意信息、集中精力。女性大脑需要较少的刺激来集中精力

• 较高的血清素值——负责大脑中的情感区域。女性大脑不太可能会忽略它的情感反应

• 较强的语言处理能力

一般来说，女性应该：
• 同时使用左右脑
• 多任务式学习，比如同时学习几个东西，或同时使用几种学习方法
• 将语言优势运用于学习
• 考虑一下学习小组

BRAIN POWER

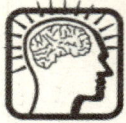

MALE & FEMALE BRAIN

The male brain has:

- Greater compartmentalisation – a tendency to use the left and right brain independently, focusing on one task at a time
- Higher levels of testosterone (10 x females) – more action oriented/competitive
- Lower levels of dopamine – the male brain needs greater stimulus to maintain attention
- Lower levels of serotonin – the male brain is more likely to override the emotional responses of the reptilian and mammalian brains
- A greater capacity devoted to visual-spatial processing

Generally, males should:

- Focus on a specific topic or task when learning
- Use a more structured learning style
- Use greater levels of stimulation to maintain their interest
- Set achievable targets for early and continued success
- Use their visual-spatial strength in learning

Notes

_____

_____

_____

_____

_____

脑力

男性和女性大脑

男性大脑有：

• 较大分工——倾向于独立地使用左脑和右脑，一次专注一项任务

• 较高的睾丸素值（女性的 10 倍）——更为行动导向、好竞争

• 较低的多巴胺值——男性大脑需要更强的刺激来集中精力

• 较低的血清素值——男性大脑更容易忽视爬虫类脑和哺乳类脑的情感反应

• 较强的视觉－空间处理能力

一般来说，男性应该：

• 学习时专注于某个特定的话题或任务
• 使用一种更有组织的学习方式
• 使用更强的刺激来维持兴趣
• 为早期和之后的成功设定可实现的目标
• 将视觉－空间方面的优势运用于学习

BRAIN POWER

LEARNING CURVE

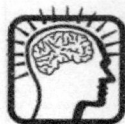

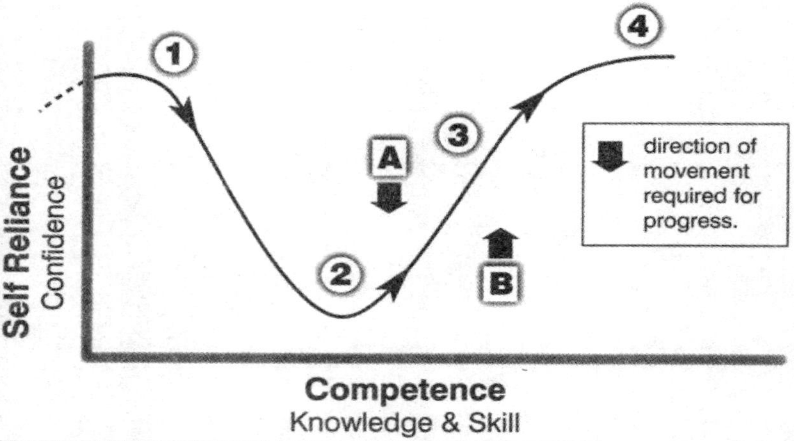
1
2
3
4
A
B
direction of movement required for progress.
Self Reliance
Confidence
Competence
Knowledge & Skill

Notes

脑力

学习曲线

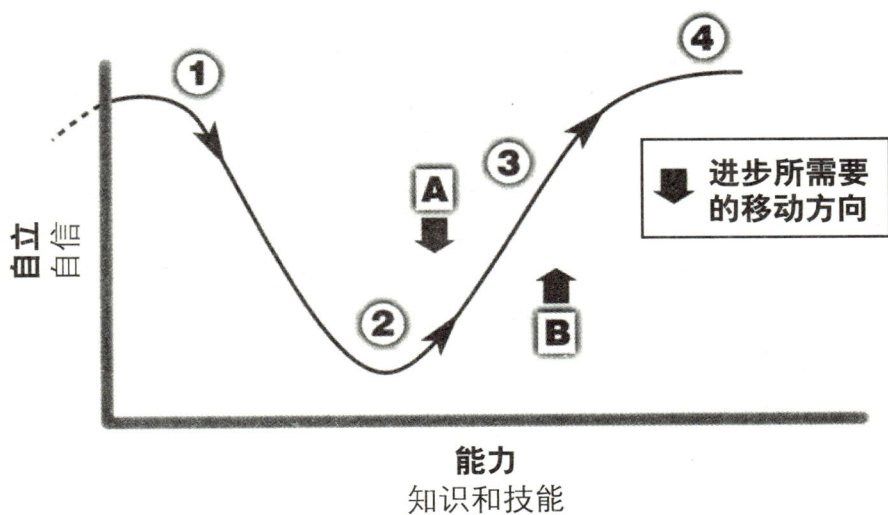

図中文字：
① ② ③ ④

自立
自信

能力
知识和技能

进步所需要
的移动方向

BRAIN POWER

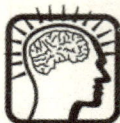

LEARNING CURVE

(1) Unconscious incompetent — Your confidence exceeds your ability, you do not know, you are not knowledgeable/skilful

(2) Conscious incompetent — Your confidence drops as you realise your ability is limited

(3) Conscious competent — Your confidence increases as your ability increases, you have to concentrate on what you know/do

(4) Unconscious competent — Your confidence and ability have peaked, you no longer have to concentrate on what you know/do; this is the start of the next learning curve. In order to learn, you must be on the curve to move forward

In different areas of your life you will be at different stages on different learning curves.

At **A** confidence exceeds ability – a drop in confidence is needed to move forward.

At **B** ability exceeds confidence – a boost in confidence is needed to move forward.

Notes

脑力

学习曲线

① **不自觉不胜任**　你的自信超过了能力，你不知道自己还没有足够的知识和技能。

② **自觉不胜任**　意识到能力有限，你的自信也下降了。

③ **自觉胜任**　能力提高，自信也增强了；你应该专注于你所知道的或是你正在做的。

④ **不自觉胜任**　你的自信和能力已经达到了顶峰，不再需要专注于你所知道的或是你正在做的；这是下一个学习曲线的开始。为了学习，你必须在曲线上不断前进。

在人生的不同时间段，你将处于不同学习曲线的不同阶段。

在 **A** 段　自信超过能力——减少过多自信才能不断前进。

在 **B** 段　能力超过自信——提升自信才能不断前进。

THE FOUR STAGES OF LEARNING

Reasoning
- Focus your mind on why you are learning
- Get in a positive frame of mind

Planning
- Break the bulk of your learning down into manageable chunks
- Plan your time and environment

Committing
- Commit yourself to learn
- Put knowledge into your brain for future use

Reflecting
- Prove to yourself you know
- Get better, for future learning

Notes

_____

_____

_____

_____

_____

脑力

学习的四个阶段

论证
· 将注意力集中于为什么学习上
· 心态乐观积极

计划
· 把学习划分为多个可管理板块
· 规划你的时间和环境

投入
· 投入学习
· 在头脑中储备知识以备将来之需

反思
· 证明给自己看你知道
· 为将来的学习做得更好

REASONING & PLANNING

论证和计划

REASONING

FOCUS THE MIND

'Why am I learning?' - **If you do not know, you will not learn.**

Remember

W hat's
I n
I t
F or
M e

W.I.F.M

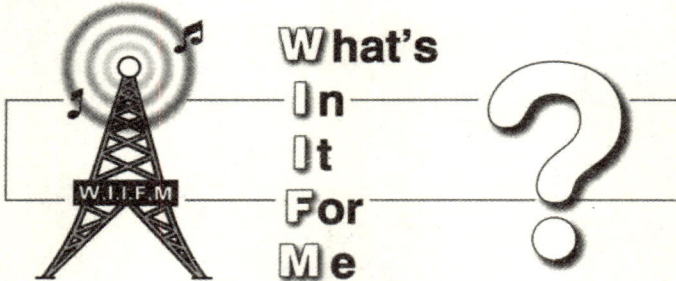

ie: Do not make your focus passing an exam or achieving a qualification.
Focus on what that qualification gives you or will do for you.

Notes

_____

_____

_____

_____

_____

集中精力

"我为什么学习？"——**如果你不知道，学习就没有效果。**

记住

例如：不要把焦点放在通过考试或取得资格上。

关心一下那份资格会给你带来什么或对你有什么帮助。

REASONING

FOCUS THE MIND

Prepare your mind for learning:

Use **POSITIVE** affirmations	'I enjoy learning' 'I learn and remember easily' 'I am a confident learner'

Visualise what success will feel and look like – use positive past experiences. Positive experiences are more easily remembered: make whatever you learn easier to remember.

For more information on goal setting, affirmations, visualisation and achieving success with your learning, see **The Personal Success Pocketbook**, also by Paul Hayden.

Notes

_____

_____

_____

_____

_____

论证

集中精力

大脑做好学习的准备：

使用 **积极的** 肯定句

"我享受学习"
"我善于学习和记忆"
"我是个自信的学习者"

想象一下成功是什么样子，有什么感觉——借鉴过去的积极经历。积极经历更容易被记住：让你更容易记住所学的东西。

要了解更多关于目标设定、积极肯定、想象以及学习中收获成功的知识，请看保罗·海登的**《个人成功》**。

PLANNING

CREATING TIME

We all have the same resource in a day – 86,400 seconds. How you invest yours is important.

Create time for learning, eg:

- Rearrange activities to free up chunks of time
- Sacrifice other activities, remember WIIFM
- Switch off the TV at the end of the programme you want to watch
- Integrate study with other areas of your life
- Sacrifice lunch breaks occasionally and grab a sandwich (do not skip lunch, just the break)
- Use travel time on buses and trains
- Carry notes/books etc to study during downtime, eg: queuing

Notes

计划

创造时间

　　一天中我们有同样的资源——86,400 秒。如何投资你的资源很重要。

　　为学习创造时间，如：

- 重新安排活动以挤出时间
- 放弃其他的活动，记住 WIIFM（它对我意味着什么？）
- 看完想看的节目后关掉电视
- 把学习和生活中其他内容结合起来
- 偶尔牺牲一下午休时间，记得拿一个三明治（不要不吃午餐，利用午休时间就好）
- 利用在公交车或火车上的时间
- 带上笔记本或书等以便在休息时学习，如排队时

STRUCTURE YOUR LEARNING

Salami Method

Does not look appealing   *until*   you slice it up

Break your learning down into manageable pieces; it makes it easier to swallow.

Backward thinking makes it easy to focus on what needs to be done daily
- Start with the end in mind
- Work back from your target/deadline date
- Spread out your slices

Notes

_____

_____

_____

_____

_____

計划

规划学习

意大利腊肠方法

毫无诱惑力　　　　　到　　　　　切成薄片，倍感诱人

把学习任务划分为一个个可规划的板块；这样更容易学习吸收。

逆向思维让你更容易专注于每天要做的事。

- 从脑海里的最终目的开始
- 从目标日期或截止日期往前工作
- 展开一个个学习板块

PLANNING

LEARNING PLAN

- Use your diary to plan your learning
- Make yourself a learning plan, mapping out blocks of time on particular days
- Plan days off as a reward
- Commit to learning on the days you have planned and enjoy the days off – do not overdo it

Experiment with various times of the day, if possible, to see when you learn best.

Notes

_____

_____

_____

_____

_____

计划

学习计划

- 用日记来做学习计划
- 制订一个学习计划：安排出特定日期的时间段
- 留出几天休息作为奖励
- 承诺在规划的日子里学习，并享受休息时间——不要过度学习

如果可能的话，在一天的不同时间段都试试，看看哪个时间段学习效果最佳。

MIND & BODY

DIET

- You would not put the wrong fuel into a high performance sports car: do not put the wrong fuel in your body and mind. Too much sugar, starch, caffeine and alcohol dull the mind. (NB: tea has more caffeine than coffee. Caffeine is a diuretic and will dehydrate you)

- Drink the recommended daily allowance of water to re-hydrate your brain. Dehydration shrivels brain cells, causing headaches and impaired creativity and memory

- Recent research by Northumbria University has shown that chewing gum has a positive effect on concentration and memory and boosts the oxygen supply to the brain

- Keep a well balanced diet. As diet has become worse, more and more people are suffering from mental illness, most commonly anxiety and depression

- While you sleep your brain still burns energy, which needs replacing. Skipping breakfast results in dullness and forgetfulness for the rest of the day

- Glucose generates the 20/25 watts of electricity the brain needs to function. The brain uses two thirds of the body's glucose. Having five or six smaller meals throughout the day maintains a more even metabolic rate, aiding concentration. Don't skip breakfast or lunch

Notes

計划

大脑与身体

饮食

· 你不会给一辆高性能跑车加错油，也不要给你的大脑和身体乱加养料。太多糖、淀粉、咖啡因和酒精会使大脑变笨。（注意：茶比咖啡含有更多的咖啡因。作为利尿剂，咖啡因会使你脱水。）

· 每天喝一定量的水给大脑补充水分。脱水会使得大脑细胞萎缩，引起头痛，损害创造力和记忆力。

· 诺森比亚大学近期一项研究表明：嚼口香糖有助于集中精力，加强记忆，加快大脑的供氧。

· 合理饮食。由于饮食变差，越来越多的人有精神问题，最普遍的是焦虑和抑郁。

· 睡觉的时候大脑仍在消耗能量，因此能量需要更新。不吃早餐会使你一天都迟钝健忘。

· 葡萄糖提供了大脑运转需要的 20/25 瓦特的电量。大脑占用了身体 2/3 的葡萄糖。一天少吃多餐五六次，新陈代谢会更加稳定，有助于精神集中。不要不吃早餐或午餐。

PLANNING

MIND & BODY
DIET – VITAMINS & MINERALS

Vitamin A – Aids vision; found in fats and oils

B Vitamins – Keep you mentally alert; found in wholegrains, seeds, lentils, yeast, nuts, eggs and milk products
Vitamin B3 is essential for proper brain functioning
Vitamin B5 and **B6** are particularly important for memory; also found in fish and chicken
Vitamin B12 is essential for the production of red blood cells, which carry oxygen. Found in animal products such as meat, milk and eggs.
Vegetarians may need to take extra as it is scarce in their diet

Vitamin C – Anti-oxidant; protects other vitamins from destruction. Also contains acetylcholine, a neural transmitter essential for short and long-term memory function; found in fresh fruit and vegetables

Vitamin E – Increases cell oxygenisation. Protects the brain against oxidised fats that slow the brain metabolism; found in wholegrains, whole wheat and sunflower seed oil

Iron – Used to transport oxygen in the blood. Remember, your brain uses 25% of your body's oxygen. Also assists in the promotion of cell and tissue growth, including in the brain; found in meat and fresh vegetables

 *Notes*

_____

_____

_____

_____

_____

计划

大脑与身体

饮食——维生素＆矿物质

维生素 A——有助于视力；多存在于动植物脂肪和食用油中。

B 族维生素——使你思维敏锐；多存在于谷物、种子、扁豆、酵母、坚果、鸡蛋和奶制品中。

维生素 B3——对大脑机能正常运作至关重要。

维生素 B5 和 **B6** 对记忆尤其重要。多存在于鸡肉和鱼肉中。

维生素 B12 对制造运送氧气的红细胞至关重要。多存在于畜产品中，比如肉类、牛奶和鸡蛋。
素食主义者应多吃维生素 B12 以补充饮食中的缺失。

维生素 C——抗氧化；保护其他维生素不受破坏。也含有乙酰胆碱。乙酰胆碱是一种神经递质，对短期和长期记忆功能至关重要；多存在于新鲜水果和蔬菜中。

维生素 E——加强细胞氧化。保护大脑免受氧化了的脂肪的破坏，这种脂肪会减缓大脑的新陈代谢；多存在于谷物、全麦和葵花籽油中。

铁——运送血液中的氧气。记住：大脑占用了身体中 25％ 的氧气。帮助加速细胞和组织的生长，包括大脑中的细胞和组织；多存在于肉类和新鲜蔬菜中。

MIND & BODY

RELAXATION

Energy for learning is released through relaxation. Before learning, bring about a calm and positive mood. Try the following:

With your eyes closed, sit and:

- Listen to relaxing music
- Tense and relax each muscle in turn, starting with your feet and working up your body
- Imagine walking down a flight of stairs; after each step exhale and say, 'I am even more relaxed now'

These exercises have a double effect as they also stimulate both sides of the brain in preparation for learning.

Sleep
Research has shown that sleep deprivation reduces your ability to learn and retain information. It also shows that on average we get one to two hours less sleep than we need. Sleep also enables your brain to process what you have learned and make sense of it.

Notes

_____

_____

_____

_____

_____

计划

大脑与身体

放松

放松之后才能获得学习的能量。学习之前，确保有个平和积极的心境。尝试以下的方法：

闭上眼睛，坐下并且：

- 听听放松的音乐
- 轮番收紧和放松肌肉，从脚开始，自下而上，放松全身肌肉。
- 想象你正在下楼梯；每下一级，呼气并且告诉自己，"我现在更放松了。"

这些练习具有双重的效果，因为它们也刺激大脑两侧为接下来的学习做准备。

睡眠

研究表明，睡眠不足会降低学习能力和信息记忆能力。研究也表明，我们的睡眠时间比实际需要的平均少一到两小时。睡眠也能帮助大脑处理和理解所学的知识。

PLANNING

MIND & BODY
EXERCISE & MOVEMENT

Movement stimulates the flow of blood and oxygen to your brain. It gives the body more sensory cues to trigger and aid recall. Motion determines emotion. The word 'emotion' comes from the Latin *movere* meaning move.

Your body language communicates the way you feel. The reverse is also true. Your body language can be used to influence the way you feel. When you are learning, sit appropriately and get up and move about regularly.

- Exercise regularly to clear the arteries and oxygenate the blood
- Remember the brain uses 25% of body's oxygen and blood supply

- Controlled rhythmic breathing results in greater brain oxidatior
- Use what exercise works best for you, but regular **rest** is also necessary for the brain to function fully

'MENS SANA IN CORPORE SANO'

A healthy mind in a healthy body

Notes

_____

_____

_____

_____

_____

计划

大脑与身体

锻炼与运动

运动会加速大脑血液的流动和供氧的消耗。它给予身体更多的感官线索，激发和辅助回忆。运动决定情绪。"情绪"一词来自拉丁词"movere"，意思是移动。

身体语言传达了你的感受。反之也是成立的。身体语言能影响你的感觉。学习时，要坐好，时不时地站起来来回走走。

• 经常锻炼有利于疏通动脉，给血液供氧。

• 有控制、有节奏的呼吸能促进大脑的氧化作用。

• 记住：大脑占用了身体25％的氧气和血液供应。

• 采用对你最有效的方式进行锻炼，但有规律的**休息**对大脑的正常运转也是很必要的。

氧气

'MENS SANA IN CORPORE SANO'

健全的精神寓于健全的身体

ENVIRONMENT

Workspace
- Should be inviting and encourage study
- Remove all distractions
- Ensure everything you need is to hand eg books, pens and paper
- Display posters and mind maps to stimulate your mind

Chair

- Comfortable and straight backed
- High enough so your feet are flat on the floor and thighs parallel to the ground
- Good posture increases supply of blood to the brain

Table/Desk
- Navel height, with as much space as necessary
- Do not cramp yourself

Temperature

- Not too warm, otherwise you relax

Notes

_____

_____

_____

_____

_____

计划

环境

工作区

- 环境应该怡人，有学习氛围
- 撤走所有会使人分心的东西
- 确保所有需要的东西都近在手边，如书、笔和纸
- 布置一些海报和思维导图以刺激你的大脑

椅子

- 舒适的直背椅
- 要足够高，这样你的脚就可以平踏在地上使大腿与地面平行
- 端正的姿势可以加速大脑的血液循环

会议桌 / 书桌

- 脐高，留出足够的空间
- 不要太束缚自己

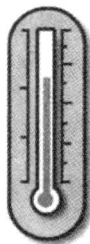

温度

- 不要太暖和，否则很容易令人放松

ENVIRONMENT

Light

- Natural light is best – sit by a window if you can
- Daylight affects your melatonin and hormone levels. These influence the release of neurotransmitters, essential to memory and alertness. The more daylight you get, the more alert you will be
- Standard bulb is better than fluorescent light

Music

- See page 176

Air

- To function well the brain needs oxygen – as clean and fresh as possible; open the nearest window
- At breaks go outside if possible
- Plants oxygenate a room, filter out harmful gases from the air and create an air of calm

Toys

- Try squeezing stress balls, playing with slinkies, fidgeting with bendy toys, etc.
- Touch stimulates the nerve endings near the skin's surface. These nerve endings send messages to the brain, keeping your brain alert

 *Notes*

计划

环境

光线

- 自然光是最好的选择——可能的话，坐在靠窗的地方
- 日光会影响你的褪黑激素和荷尔蒙水平。这些会影响神经递质的释放，而神经递质对记忆力和灵敏度至关重要。接受的日光越多，人就会变得越机警
- 标准灯泡比荧光灯要好

空气

- 大脑的运转需要干净、新鲜的氧气；打开离你最近的窗户
- 休息时，尽可能地去室外
- 植物会在房间里释放氧气，滤除空气里的有害气体，形成一个使人平静的氛围

音乐

- 见 177 页。

玩具

- 试一试挤压应力球，玩一玩弹簧玩具，摆弄摆弄柔韧玩具等
- 触摸会刺激表皮附近的神经末梢。这些神经末梢给大脑传递信息，保持大脑的灵敏

ENVIRONMENT

FRAGRANCE & LEARNING

Dr Alan Hirsch of the Smell and Taste Research Foundation in Chicago noted an increase from 14% to 54% for students in a calculus exam, when they were exposed to a floral aroma. The sense of smell has unfiltered, quicker access to the brain than any of the other senses. It can raise attention and awareness levels dramatically. Think of freshly baked bread or fresh coffee.

Here is a list of the characteristics of various aromas:

Grapefruit   Radiating, cheerful, liberating
Lemon   Stimulating, clarifying, concentration-building
Narcissus   Empowering, visionary, creative
Peppermint   Clarifying, awakening, stimulating, refreshing
Sandalwood   Enlightening, balancing, connecting
Thyme   Empowering, assisting, invigorating

(See further: The Fragrant Mind by aromatherapist Valerie Ann Worwood.)

Consider using scented gel pens or markers to introduce colour and scent to your learning.

Notes

_____

_____

_____

_____

_____

计划

环境

香气与学习

芝加哥嗅觉与味觉研究基金会的艾伦·赫希博士发现，在有花香的情况下，学生微积分考试的成绩都有14％～54％的提升。嗅觉不经任何过滤，比其他任何一种感觉都能更快地进入大脑。它可以极大地提高注意力和警觉心。想一想新鲜出炉的面包或咖啡。

下面是各种香气的特征列表：

葡萄柚　　散热，使人感到愉悦，对人有益
柠檬　　　刺激作用，净化作用，使人集中精力
水仙　　　赋予人力量，使人有远见，有创造力
胡椒薄荷　使人清醒，唤醒作用，刺激作用，提神作用
檀香　　　启发，平衡，连接
百里香　　赋予人力量，协助作用，鼓舞作用

（参见芳香理疗师瓦勒莉·安·沃伍德的著作《芳香疗法配方宝典》）

试试用一下香味圆珠笔或者记号笔，将颜色和香味带入你的学习。

PLANNING

RE-FOCUS

When you are ready to start learning, re-focus.

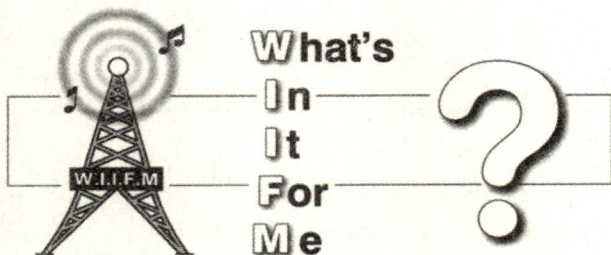

What's
In
It
For
Me

W.I.I.F.M

?

'Why am I learning?'

Notes

_____

_____

_____

_____

_____

计划

重定焦点

"准备好学习的时候，开始重定焦点。

它对我意味着什么？

"我为什么学习？"

COMMITTING

投 入

STARTING FROM SCRATCH?

BEFORE BEGINNING TO LEARN

- Write down key headings/words of what you already know, or use a mind map to provide the links for the new information.

- In the unlikely event you know absolutely nothing:
  - Read the appropriate section of an encyclopedia, or
  - Read a book aimed at children; these are especially good as they are simple and have plenty of pictures to stimulate the right brain too

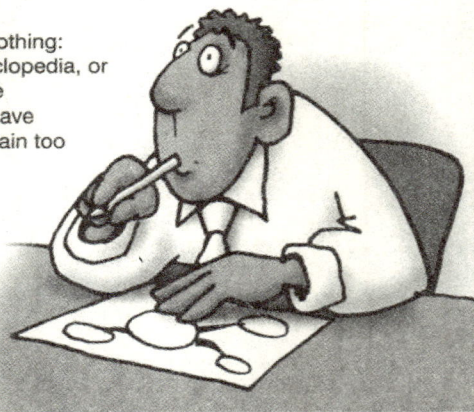

- Use brain gym exercises (see next page)

 *Notes*

_____

_____

_____

_____

_____

投入

从头开始？

开始学习之前

• 写下重点标题、已经认识的单词，或是使用思维导图来提供新信息间的联系

• 假如遇到了什么都不知道的情况：
——查阅百科全书相关部分；
——或者阅读针对儿童的书籍，这些书简单并且配有大量的图片，这些图片能刺激右脑，对你帮助很大

• 多做脑力健身操锻炼（参见下一页）

COMMITTING

BRAIN GYM

These are warm up activities to prepare the brain for learning and/or as energisers during learning. If the brain is warmed up, the information being learned will be retained more effectively.

A warm up can include a recap on existing knowledge and activities that stimulate both hemispheres of the brain. The ideal study time for an adult is 20–30 minutes but taking a break every half hour may be disruptive. Instead use a brain gym exercise to re-energise yourself.

Brain gym exercises also stimulate alpha brainwaves. This induces the ideal state for learning.

Brain gym exercises

- Logic problems
- Memory games
- Brain teasers
- Rebus
- Pat your tummy and rub your head
- Juggling
- Quick puzzles
- Recite the alphabet backwards

Notes

_____

_____

_____

_____

_____

投入

脑力健身操

　　这些热身活动能帮助大脑做好学习的准备，或者被用作学习过程中的兴奋剂。如果大脑准备运动做好了，学到的信息就能被更有效地记住。

　　大脑准备活动可以包括复习已经学过的知识或是做些能刺激大脑左右两个半球的活动。成人的理想学习时间是 20 至 30 分钟，但是每半小时休息一次是不利于学习效果的。你可以做做脑力健身操来振奋精神。

　　脑力健身操锻炼也可以刺激 α 波，这能激发理想的学习状态。

脑力健身操锻炼

- 逻辑问题
- 记忆游戏
- 脑筋急转弯
- 字谜

- 拍拍你的肚子，摸摸你的头
- 玩杂耍
- 快速拼图
- 倒背字母表

COMMITTING

THE SIX W'S

BEFORE BEGINNING TO LEARN

Create an interest in the material to be learned. Remember – interest creates motivation to learn and aids retention.

Ask questions that you want answered by your study.

W ho?   Who discovered this? Who are the key characters?
W hat?   What are the counter arguments? What are the key facts?
W hen?   When was this discovered? When did this happen?
W here?   Where did this happen? Where was he/she born?
W hy?   Why did this happen? Why should I believe this?
Ho**W**?   How will this work? How does this relate to my existing knowledge?

If you are not asking questions you are not learning.

Notes

_____

_____

_____

_____

_____

投入

六个 W

开始学习之前

对将要学习的材料充满兴趣。记住：兴趣能激发学习动力，帮助记忆。

提出一些你想通过自己的学习解决的问题。

谁？	（Who）	谁发现了这个？谁是主要角色？
什么？	（What）	反面论证是什么？关键事实是什么？
什么时候？	（When）	什么时间发现的？什么时候发生的？
什么地点？	（Where）	在哪里发生的？他或她出生在哪里？
为什么？	（Why）	为什么发生？为什么我应该相信？
怎么样？	（How）	这个效果怎么样？这怎么与我已有的知识联系起来？

不会提问就不会学习。

KOLB'S CIRCULAR LEARNING THEORY

David Kolb developed an experiential learning theory:

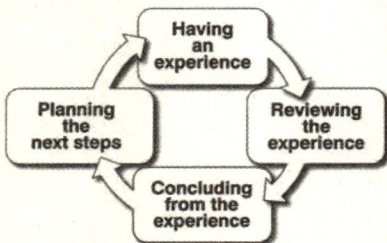

Kolb's theory was built around two dimensions:

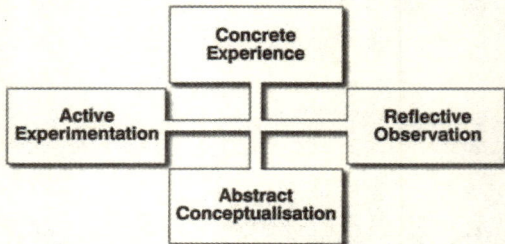

His theory is that effective learning requires the use of all four abilities. Few people are equally balanced, most tend to develop a strength, or preference. Using only your preferred style can put you at a serious disadvantage.

Notes

投入

库伯的循环学习理论

大卫·库伯提出了经验
学习理论：

库伯的理论有两个方面：

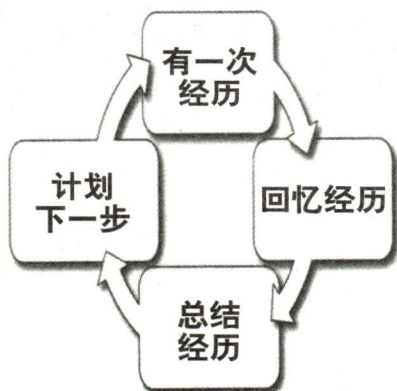

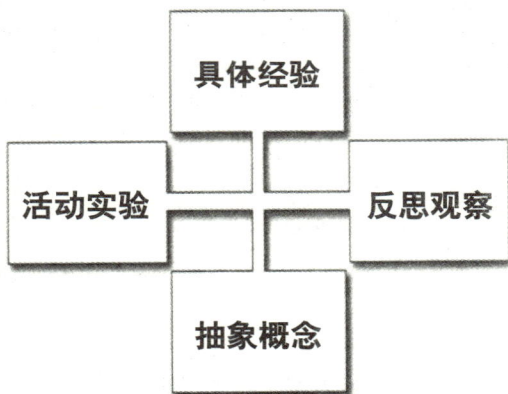

他的理论认为，有效学习要求使用以上所有四种能力。很少有人能平衡这四种能力，大多数人都有一种优势或偏好。仅仅使用你喜欢的模式会对你不利。

COMMITTING

HONEY AND MUMFORD'S LEARNING STYLES
ACTIVISTS

Peter Honey and Alan Mumford built on Kolb's work, developing four learning styles. The following will help you identify your preferred style, get the most from it and show you how to develop a more rounded style:

Activists – Preference for active experimentation (Philosophy: 'I'll try anything once')

Activists:
- Involve themselves fully and without bias in new experiences
- Tackle things with a *have a go* mentality
- Enjoy and live in the here and now
- Don't need detail
- Are open minded/optimistic, love anything new
- Act first and consider the consequences later

- Can take risks for the sake of it
- Thrive on new challenges but get bored quickly
- Are extrovert, enjoy group activities and performing to a crowd
- May become glory seekers
- Are not good at finishing
- May find training sessions too slow

Notes

_____

_____

_____

_____

_____

投入

霍尼和芒福德的学习模式

积极分子

彼得·霍尼和艾伦·芒福德借鉴库伯的理论发展了四种学习模式。阅读下面的内容，它能帮你识别自己的偏好模式，最大限度地利用它，并且告诉你如何培养一种更全面的模式。

> **积极分子**——偏好活动实验（理念："我会尝试任何事物。"）

积极分子：

- 积极参与，对新体验没有任何偏见
- 对事物抱有一种"试试"的心态
- 活在当下，享受此刻
- 不需要细节
- 思想开放、乐观，喜欢新事物
- 先行动再考虑后果
- 可以为此承担风险
- 面对新挑战很兴奋，但是很快就厌倦了
- 外向，喜欢小组活动，乐于在群体前表现
- 可能会追求荣誉
- 很难做到善始善终
- 可能会觉得培训课程进度太慢

COMMITTING

HONEY AND MUMFORD'S LEARNING STYLES
ACTIVISTS

You learn **best** from activities that:
- Have elements of *have a go* and offer short *here and now* exercises and games
- Provide new experiences and opportunities to learn from
- Allow you to get involved with others, eg solving problems as a team
- Have assorted activities to tackle, that change quickly, are challenging and provide opportunities for glory
- Present you with the opportunity to be in the limelight, eg as a spokesperson for your group, facilitate a discussion

You learn **least** from activities that:
- Require you to be passive, eg reading, listening to a presentation
- Involve solitary work
- Repeat the same routine and predictable tasks including excessive practising
- Demand attention to detail, a thorough job and analysis of data
- Give you little room for movement because they are so precise

Notes

_____

_____

_____

_____

_____

投入

霍尼和芒福德的学习模式

积极分子

从以下活动中，你的学习收获**最多**：

- 有尝试的元素，有此时此地的锻炼和游戏
- 给人新的体验和机会从中学习
- 有和别人打交道的机会，比如以团队的形式解决问题
- 有各种各样迅速变化的活动，有挑战性，有获得荣誉的机会
- 有成为公众瞩目中心的机会，比如作为你的小组发言人，开展讨论

从以下活动中，你**很难**学到东西：

- 处于被动位置，比如读书、听报告
- 有单独作业
- 重复着同样的事情、可预测的任务，包括过度练习
- 要求注意细节，仔细的工作和分析数据
- 因为要求精确，所以你很难有自己发挥的空间

COMMITTING

HONEY AND MUMFORD'S LEARNING STYLES
REFLECTORS

> **Reflectors** – Preference for reflective observation (Philosophy – 'Let me think about this')

Reflectors:

- Prefer to stand back to ponder experiences and consider them from many angles
- Prefer to collect information from different sources and consider alternatives before coming to a conclusion
- Are happy to deal with detail
- Are cautious and thoughtful
- Are holistic – like to look at all sides of the picture
- Are unable to make quick decisions
- Take a back seat in meetings and debates
- Enjoy observing other people in action
- Listen to others' points of view before making their own points
- Enjoy discussing and putting things into perspective
- Adopt a low profile and have slightly detatched, aloof, calm characters
- Are happy to work behind the scenes
- Prepare well
- May find training sessions too fast

Notes

投入

霍尼和芒福德的学习模式

反思者

> **反思者**——偏好反思观察（理念："让我思考一下。"）

反思者：

- 喜欢退一步思考经历，从多方面考虑
- 喜欢多渠道收集信息，得出结论前会考虑备选项
- 乐于处理细节
- 细心、深思熟虑
- 从整体着眼——喜欢考虑事情的所有方面
- 不能快速做出决定
- 会议和辩论中会坐在后面
- 喜欢观察别人的行动
- 发表自己的观点前，先听别人的观点
- 喜欢讨论，全面地观察事物
- 低调，性格稍稍有点不合群，超然、镇静
- 喜欢幕后工作
- 做好充分准备
- 可能会觉得培训课程进度太快

COMMITTING

HONEY AND MUMFORD'S LEARNING STYLES
REFLECTORS

You learn **best** from activities that:
- Encourage you to watch, listen and think, eg observing a roleplay or watching a video
- Allow you time to think and prepare fully, before you decide/act
- Use activities such as research, observation, analysis of data and regular reviews
- Get you to produce considered and measured analyses and reports
- Allow you to exchange thought out views in a low-risk environment
- Offer opportunities for feedback

You learn **least** from activities that:
- Force you into the limelight, eg roleplays, particularly if they allow no planning time
- Get you doing something without warning, eg to give an instant reaction or idea
- Have restrictive timeframes, fast pace or rush you from one exercise to the next
- Have poor communication and information flow, requiring you to make decisions with insufficient information, eg a badly briefed exercise on a training course
- Give no opportunity for reviews or feedback

Notes

投入

霍尼和芒福德的学习模式

反思者

从以下活动中，你的学习收获**最多**：

- 鼓励你去看、去听、去思考，比如观察一场角色扮演表演或是看一段录像
- 在做决定或行动之前，给你充分的时间思考和准备
- 活动中涉及调查、观察、数据分析和定期回顾
- 需要你做深思熟虑的、慎重的分析和报告
- 能够在低风险的环境下交流深思熟虑的观点
- 有得到反馈的机会

从以下活动中，你**很难**学到东西：

- 迫使你处在中心位置，比如角色扮演，尤其是没有给你任何准备时间的时候
- 在没有任何事先通知的情况下让你做某事，比如立刻做出反应或是给出主意
- 时间紧迫，节奏快，让你做完一个练习马上就做下一个
- 交流少，信息流动少，要求你在信息不足的情况下作出决定，比如一个培训课程上介绍不到位的练习
- 很少有机会去做回顾或是看反馈

COMMITTING

HONEY AND MUMFORD'S LEARNING STYLES
THEORISTS

Theorists – Preference for abstract conceptualisation (Philosophy – 'What's the relationship?')

Theorists:
- Assimilate and adapt observations and abstract ideas into complex yet logically sound and coherent theories
- Are reluctant to test theories in practice
- Think problems through in a step-by-step rational, logical way but can over-complicate
- Only produce prepared ideas – low risk takers
- Are perfectionists who won't rest until things fit into a rational scheme
- Like to investigate and integrate
- Comfortable with principles, theories, models and systems

- Prefer to work alone and take their time
- Prefer rational objectivity to subjective ambiguity
- Are uncomfortable with lateral thinking and anything flippant
- Have the patience for complexities
- May have an ivory tower image
- Ask questions probing basic assumptions

Notes

_____

_____

_____

_____

_____

投入

霍尼和芒福德的学习模式

理论家

> **理论家**——偏好抽象概念（理念——"关系是什么？"）

理论家：

- 吸收观察到的信息和抽象观点，并把它们改编成复杂、但逻辑上合理和连贯的理论
- 不愿意在实践中测试理论
- 一步步地、合理有逻辑地思考问题，但是可能会使问题过于复杂
- 只会给出自己准备好的想法，不愿意冒风险
- 完美主义者，直到事情变得合理有序才会休息
- 喜欢调查、整合
- 适应原则、理论、模式和系统之类

- 喜欢独自不紧不慢地工作
- 喜欢合理的客观性，而不是主观的模棱两可
- 不喜欢横向思维和浮躁的东西
- 对复杂的东西有耐心
- 可能会给人一种在象牙塔中的印象
- 提一些探讨基本假设的问题

COMMITTING

HONEY AND MUMFORD'S LEARNING STYLES
THEORISTS

You learn **best** from activities that:
- Use, or are part of, a model, theory or philosophy
- Give you time to explore thoroughly and logically the links, relationships and associations
- Allow you to investigate underpinning fundamentals, logic or theory
- Stretch you intellectually, eg analysing, debating or participating in complex situations to test your understanding
- Provide clear guidelines, structure and purpose
- Give you valuable concepts, even if they are not relevant
- Involve well argued, watertight debate

You learn **least** from activities that:
- Are vague or uncertain and lack structure, context or reason
- Put emphasis on feelings and emotions, eg some teambuilding events
- Are results and action oriented, especially against tight deadlines
- Skim the surface, offering a high level view, without depth or substance
- Have contradictory methods/principles

Notes

_____

_____

_____

_____

_____

投入

霍尼和芒福德的学习模式

理论家

从以下活动中，你的学习收获**最多**：

• 运用一种模式、理论或哲学，或者使这些活动本身成为模式、理论或哲学的一部分
• 给你时间仔细地、有逻辑地探寻其中的联系和关系
• 让你调查基本原则、逻辑或理论
• 开发你的智力，比如分析、辩论或是参与复杂的情境来测试你的理解力
• 提供清晰的指导方针、结构和目的
• 给你有价值的概念，即使是不相关的
• 参与论据充分的、无懈可击的辩论

从以下活动中，你**很难**学到东西：

• 模糊、不确定，没有结构、背景、推理
• 强调感觉和情感，比如某些团队建设活动
• 以结果和行动为导向，尤其反对很紧的最后期限
• 触及表面，给出高层次的观点，没有深度和实质内容
• 彼此矛盾的方法和原则

HONEY AND MUMFORD'S LEARNING STYLES
PRAGMATISTS

Pragmatists – Preference for concrete experience (Philosophy – 'What would happen if...')

Pragmatists:
- Are keen to try out new ideas, theories and techniques to see if they work in practice
- Have a commonsense, practical approach to making things work
- Like trial and error
- Positively search out new ideas and take the first opportunity to experiment with applications
- Need some detail – only if they think it relevant and useful
- Impatient with reflecting, open-ended discussions and theory
- Prefer to get straight to the point in a discussion, they say what they think
- Like to get things done efficiently
- Will break rules if there is a better way to do things
- Are problem solvers – produce spontaneous ideas
- May make hasty decisions
- See problems and opportunities as a challenge

Notes

_____

_____

_____

_____

_____

投入

霍尼和芒福德的学习模式

实用主义者

实用主义者——偏好具体经验（理念——"如果那样会发生什么"）

实用主义者：

- 喜欢试验新想法、理论和技术以检测它们是否在实践中有效
- 有常识，有实用的方法
- 喜欢反复试验
- 积极寻找新想法，抓住一切机会实践运用
- 需要一些细节，但必须是他们认为相关和有用的
- 对反思、开放讨论和理论会感到不耐烦

- 喜欢在讨论中直奔重点，想什么就说什么
- 喜欢有效率地办事
- 如果有更好的做事方法的话，会打破常规
- 善于解决问题，临时会突发奇想
- 可能会草率做决定
- 把难题和机遇当做挑战

COMMITTING

HONEY AND MUMFORD'S LEARNING STYLES
PRAGMATISTS

You learn **best** from activities that:
- Give you a model to copy, eg a demonstration before you have a go, examples and stories that illustrate the point
- Allow you to practise with feedback from someone with proven credibility
- Have a clear and practical link between the learning and the application
- Present an immediate opportunity to implement the learning
- Offer clear practical benefits, eg learning how to learn

You learn **least** from activities that:
- Bear no resemblance to reality, eg some training games
- Do not offer you any benefits, eg saving, gain, guarantees
- Offer no opportunity for you to practise
- Are not able to be implemented quickly or that have barriers to implementation, eg management, red tape, procedures
- Have a high cost of failure

Notes

投入

霍尼和芒福德的学习模式

实用主义者

从以下活动中，你的学习收获**最多**：

• 给你一个模型去模仿，比如做之前给你一个演示或是阐释观点的例子或故事
• 允许你利用可靠人士的反馈来练习
• 学习和运用之间有清晰和实际的联系
• 立即给你机会来运用你的所学
• 给你清晰的、实用的好处，比如学会如何学习

从以下活动中，你**很难**学到东西：

• 和现实没有任何相似点，比如一些培训游戏
• 没有提供任何福利，比如储蓄、收益或是保障
• 没有提供任何练习的机会
• 无法快速实施，或是有实施的阻碍，比如管理、繁文缛节或程序
• 失败会付出很高代价

COMMITTING

LEARNING STYLES
THREE KINDS OF MEMORY

Your brain receives information and remembers it through the five **senses**:
- Sight (visual memory)
- Touch (kinaesthetic memory)
- Sound (auditory memory)
- Taste (gustatory memory)
- Smell (olfactory memory)

Learning studies have identified three primary kinds of memory:
Visual, **Auditory** and **Kinaesthetic**

Visual learners find it easier to take in new information through pictures, diagrams, charts, films, etc

Auditory learners find it easier to take in new information through the spoken word

Kinaesthetic learners find it easier to take in new information through copying demonstrations and getting physically involved

Controlled by the Neocortex, see page 8.

Notes

_____

_____

_____

_____

_____

投入

学习方式

三种记忆

你的大脑通过以下五种**感官**接受并记住信息：

- 视力（视觉记忆）
- 触摸（动觉记忆）
- 声音（听觉记忆）

- 味道（味觉记忆）
- 气味（嗅觉记忆）

学习研究总结出了三种基本记忆，即**视觉**、**听觉**和**动觉**。

视觉学习者们发现通过图片、图表、表格和电影更容易接受新信息。

听觉学习者们发现通过声音更容易接受新信息。

动觉学习者们发现通过模仿演示、身体上的参与，更容易接受新信息。

这受新脑皮层控制，参见第 9 页。

COMMITTING

LEARNING STYLES
THREE KINDS OF MEMORY

The best learning takes place using all three memories, eg:

If you are reading:
- Visualise the key messages
- Read aloud or hear the words internally
- Get physically involved – underline, highlight, mind map, etc

Use all three styles to **V.A.K.** up knowledge.

Learners dominate in one style and have a preference
for another. Previous learning may have been hindered
if it did not cater for your learning style. (Typically,
schools are not geared to kinaesthetic learners.)

Research has proven that 29% of learners are
primarily visual, 34% are primarily auditory and
37% are primarily kinaesthetic. Assess your
style on the following pages and use your
preferred style(s) to learn, using the
following tips.

Notes

_____

_____

_____

_____

_____

投入

学习方式

三种记忆

同时使用三种记忆会达到最好的学习效果。

比如读书时：
- 可视化关键信息
- 大声朗读或心里默读
- 让身体也动起来——划重点，思维导图等

使用所有三种方式来**学习**知识。

学习者们以一种方式为主，同时偏好另一种。如果之前的学习与你的学习方式不契合的话，之前的学习效果可能就会受到不利影响。（一般来说，学校不适合动觉学习者。）

研究表明，29％的学习者属于视觉型学习者，34％的学习者属于听觉型，37％的学习者属于动觉型。根据下面几页的内容来评估你的学习方式。借鉴下面的小建议，结合你偏好的方式来学习。

COMMITTING

LEARNING STYLES
VISUAL LEARNERS

- Use phrases such as 'I **see** what you mean', 'That **looks** right'
- When relaxing, prefer to watch a film or video, go to the theatre or read
- Prefer to talk to people face to face
- Are fast talkers, dislike listening to others
- Forget names, remember faces
- If lost or need directions, prefer a map
- When inactive, tend to doodle or watch someone/something
- When angry, are silent and seethe
- Reward people with a note, letter or card
- Are well dressed, tidy and organised

LEARN BEST BY:

- Writing down key facts or, better still, making mind maps
- Visualising what they are learning by creating pictures/diagrams
- Using time lines, for remembering dates
- Creating their own strong visual links
- Using pictures, diagrams, charts, film, video, graphics, etc

Notes

_____

_____

_____

_____

_____

投入

学习方式

视觉学习者

- 会使用这样一些短语，比如"我**看懂**（明白）你的意思了"，"**看起来**不错"
- 放松的时候，喜欢看电影或录像，去剧院，或者阅读
- 喜欢和人面对面地交流
- 喜欢夸夸其谈，不喜欢倾听
- 记不住名字，但记得住脸
- 迷路或是需要方向指导的时候，倾向于看地图
- 不活动的时候，喜欢乱写乱画、看别人或看东西
- 生气的时候会不说话、生闷气
- 会给别人写便条、信或是卡片
- 穿着考究，干净、有条理

运用以下方法会学得最好：

- 记下关键事实，或者最好是做思维导图
- 通过画图和绘制图表形象地展示所学内容
- 用时间轴来记日期
- 建立他们自己的强视觉联系
- 使用图片、图表、表格、电影、录像、制图学等

COMMITTING

LEARNING STYLES
AUDITORY LEARNERS

- Use phrases such as 'That **sounds** right', 'I **hear** what you are saying'
- When relaxing, listen to music or radio
- Prefer to talk to people on the phone
- Enjoy listening to others, but impatient to talk; talk in a rhythmic voice
- Forget faces, remember names
- If lost or need directions, prefer to be told
- When inactive, tend to talk to themselves or others
- When angry, express themselves in outbursts
- Reward people with oral praise
- Do not like reading books or instruction manuals

LEARN BEST BY:

- Hearing a seminar, presentation or explanation
- Reading aloud to themselves with emotion or accent
- Making a tape of key points to listen to in the car, while ironing, etc
- Verbally summarising in their own words
- Explaining the subject to someone else
- Use their own internal voice to verbalise what they are learning

Notes

投入

学习方式

听觉学习者

- 常会说这样一些话，比如"**听起来**不错"，"我**听到**你说的话了"
- 放松时听听音乐或广播
- 偏好与人电话聊天
- 喜欢倾听，不喜欢讲话；说话时声音富有节奏感
- 记得住名字，记不住脸
- 迷路或需要方向指导时，喜欢问路
- 不活动时，喜欢自言自语或找人说话
- 生气时，会大吼大叫来发泄
- 会口头赞美别人
- 不喜欢阅读图书或是指导手册之类

采用以下方式学习效果最好：

- 听研讨会、报告或是讲解
- 有情感、带口音地大声朗读
- 把重点内容录成磁带在车上或是熨衣服的时候听
- 口头上用自己的话总结
- 向别人介绍主题
- 心里默念所学内容

COMMITTING

LEARNING STYLES
KINAESTHETIC LEARNERS

- Use phrases such as 'I found it easy to **handle**', 'That **touched** a nerve'
- When relaxing, prefer to play games and sport
- Prefer to talk to people while doing something else
- Slow talkers, use gestures and expressions
- Shake hands with people they meet
- If lost or need directions, prefer to be shown the way
- When inactive, cannot sit still for long
- When angry, clench their fists, grit their teeth and storm off
- Reward people with a pat on the back

LEARN BEST BY:

- Copying demonstrations
- Making models
- Recording information as they hear it, preferably in a mind map
- Walking around while they read
- Underlining/highlighting new information/key points
- Putting key points on to index cards and sorting them into order
- Getting physically and actively involved in their learning

Notes

投入

学习方式

动觉学习者

- 常会说这样一些话，比如"我觉得这很容易**处理**""那**触及**要害了"
- 放松时，喜欢玩游戏或做运动
- 喜欢一边做事一边和人说话
- 讲话很慢，喜欢用手势和表情
- 会和遇见的人握手
- 当迷路或需要方向指导时，喜欢找人指路
- 闲着时，没有耐心长时间静坐
- 生气时，会握拳、咬牙、怒冲冲地离开
- 感谢别人时，会拍拍别人的背

采用以下方式学习效果最好：

- 模仿演示
- 做模型
- 听到信息时，借助思维导图记住它们
- 读书时四处走动
- 在新信息或重点下面划线或着重强调
- 把重点写在索引卡上，并按序分类
- 积极投入学习，学习时身体也动起来

EIGHT OR MORE INTELLIGENCES

The concept of multiple intelligences was first discovered by Professor Howard Gardner of Harvard University in 1983. His ground-breaking book, *Frames of Mind* redefined beliefs on human intelligence. Gardner's research originally introduced seven intelligences. He was able to accurately pinpoint the area of the brain that correlated to each of these intelligences. In 1999 he qualified and added an eighth: Naturalistic Intelligence.

Linguistic Intelligence – used for reading, writing and speech

Logical-Mathematical Intelligence – used for Maths, logic and systems

$$\sqrt{8^2}$$

Visual-Spatial Intelligence – used for visualisation and art

Musical Intelligence – used for rhythm, music and lyrics

Notes

投入

八种或更多智能

多元智能的概念是 1983 年哈佛大学的教授霍华德·加德纳提出的。他的开创性著作《智能的结构》重新定义了人类的智能。他的研究最初介绍了七种智能。他能够精准定位大脑中与这些智能相关联的区域。1999 年，他又新增了第八种智能——自然观察智能。

语言智能：读、写、说的能力

逻辑—数理智能：运算和推理的能力 $\sqrt{8^2}$

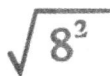

视觉—空间智能：感受视觉空间，并把所感觉到的表现出来的能力

音乐智能：感受节奏、音乐和歌词的能力

COMMITTING

EIGHT OR MORE INTELLIGENCES

Bodily-Kinaesthetic Intelligence – used for touch and reflex

Interpersonal Intelligence – used for communicating with others

Intrapersonal Intelligence – used for self-discovery and self-analysis

Naturalistic Intelligence – used for making sense of the natural world

In addition, Gardner and his colleagues also suggest the following intelligences may exist:
*Spiritual intelligence *Moral intelligence *Digital intelligence, and most convincingly,
they argue there is *Existential intelligence – a concern with ultimate issues.

The following pages are based on and adapted from their research.

Notes

投入

八种或更多智能

身体——运动智能：触摸和反应的能力

人际交流智能：与人沟通交往的能力

内省智能：自我发现和自我分析的能力

自然探索智能：感知自然环境的特征的能力

　　此外，加德纳和他的同事们还提出了以下几种智能存在的可能性：精神智能、道德智能和数字智能。此外，他们极力支持存在智能，这是一种陈述、思考有关生与死和终极世界的倾向性的能力。

　　以下几页都来源于和改编自他们的研究。

EIGHT OR MORE INTELLIGENCES

Everyone possesses all the intelligences to some extent.

The most powerful learning combines all of them.

All intelligences are of value, you need to identify where your strengths lie and use those intelligences.

Whether these are intelligences or abilities, as Professor Howard Gardner puts it, 'Multiple intelligence education is multiple chance learning'.

Assess your strengths ❏ on the following pages and use them by combining the different learning techniques.

Notes

_____

_____

_____

_____

_____

投入

八种或更多智能

每个人都或多或少拥有这八种智能。

最有效的学习是把所有这八种智能结合起来使用。

每一种智能都是有价值的。你需要辨别你的优势所在，并利用这些智能。

正如霍华德·加德纳教授所说的那样，不论这些是智能还是能力，"多元智能教育就是多种机会学习"。

根据下面的内容判断你的优势，并结合不同的学习技巧充分发挥你的优势。

COMMITTING

EIGHT OR MORE INTELLIGENCES
LINGUISTIC INTELLIGENCE

- Used for reading, writing and speech

Characteristics:
- ❑ Extensive vocabulary, good at spelling
- ❑ Good verbal and/or written communication
- ❑ Expressive, fluent talker, gives clear explanations
- ❑ Good listener
- ❑ Reasoning ability
- ❑ Methodical

Likes:
- ❑ Reading books/magazines/newspapers
- ❑ Word games/crosswords/scrabble
- ❑ Word play/puns/tongue twisters
- ❑ Theatre, radio
- ❑ Poetry
- ❑ Debate
- ❑ Writing letters

English and History were favourite subjects at school.

Notes

投入

八种或更多智能

语言智能

· 说、读、写的能力

特点：

☐ 词汇量大，擅长拼写

☐ 擅长口头交流或书面交流，
　或两者都擅长

☐ 善表达，说话流利，解释
　清晰明了

☐ 好的听众

☐ 推理能力

☐ 做事有条理

喜欢：

☐ 阅读图书、杂志、报纸

☐ 猜字游戏、纵横字谜、拼字
　游戏

☐ 文字游戏、双关语、绕口令

☐ 戏剧、广播

☐ 诗歌

☐ 辩论

☐ 写信

在学校最喜欢英语和历史。

COMMITTING

EIGHT OR MORE INTELLIGENCES
LINGUISTIC INTELLIGENCE

Learning techniques:

- Learn from books, tapes, lectures, presentations, seminars, etc
- Write down questions you want answered before starting any learning
- Read out loud
- After reading a piece of text, summarise in your own words out loud and write it down
- Always put things into your own words
- Brainstorm to organise thoughts into order and/or key points
- Write key points on cards and sort into order
- Make up crosswords and puzzles to solve (why not do this with your learning set?)
- Debate and discuss issues (preferably with your learning set)
- Present what you have learned orally or in writing to someone else (your learning set?)

Notes

_____

_____

_____

_____

_____

投入

八种或更多智能

语言智能

学习技巧：

- 从书本、磁带、讲座、报告、研讨会中学习知识
- 学习之前先写下你想要得到答案的问题
- 大声朗读
- 阅读文本之后，用自己的话大声总结并且记录下来
- 总是用自己的话来表达
- 用头脑风暴来整理想法或是列出重点
- 把重点记录在卡片上并整理排序
- 编一些纵横字谜或是智力测验题（为什么不和你的学习小组一起做呢？）
- 辩论、讨论问题（最好是和你的学习小组一起）
- 向别人口头陈述你学过的东西或是写给别人（你的学习小组？）看

COMMITTING

EIGHT OR MORE INTELLIGENCES
LOGICAL-MATHEMATICAL INTELLIGENCE

- Used for Maths, logic and systems

Characteristics:
- ☐ Good at budgeting
- ☐ Logical thought, explanation and action
- ☐ Organised, organises tasks into sequence
- ☐ Plans time and journeys effectively
- ☐ Reasoning ability
- ☐ Seeks patterns and relationships
- ☐ Precise

Likes:
- ☐ Calculations, eg dart scores, gambling odds, etc
- ☐ Solving puzzles/brain teasers requiring logical thinking
- ☐ Putting together a detailed itinerary for holidays and business trips
- ☐ Abstract thought
- ☐ Experimenting
- ☐ Scientific advances
- ☐ Computers

Maths and Science were favourite subjects at school.

Notes

_____

_____

_____

_____

投入

八种或更多智能

逻辑—数理智能

• 数学运算和逻辑推理的能力

特点：

- ☐ 擅长预算
- ☐ 逻辑思维、解释和行动
- ☐ 有条理，有次序地安排任务
- ☐ 有效地计划时间和旅行
- ☐ 推理能力
- ☐ 寻求模式和关系
- ☐ 精准

喜欢：

- ☐ 计算，比如飞镖计分、赌博胜算等
- ☐ 解决需要逻辑思考的智力测试和脑筋急转弯
- ☐ 为度假和出差做详细的行程表
- ☐ 抽象思维
- ☐ 实验
- ☐ 了解科学进展情况
- ☐ 计算机

在学校时最喜欢数学和科学。

EIGHT OR MORE INTELLIGENCES
LOGICAL-MATHEMATICAL INTELLIGENCE

Learning techniques:

- List key points in order and number them
- Use a flow chart to express information/knowledge in easy to follow steps
- Use mind maps
- Use computers, eg spreadsheets
- Experiment with the knowledge
- Use timelines for remembering dates and events
- Analyse and interpret data
- Use your reasoning and deductive skills
- Create and solve problems (this can be done with your learning set)
- Play mathematical games (this can be done with your learning set)

Notes

_____

_____

_____

_____

_____

投入

八种或更多智能

逻辑—数理智能

学习技巧：

- 有序地列出重点并编上序号
- 采用流程图来展示信息和知识以方便按步骤进行工作
- 使用思维导图
- 使用电脑，比如电子数据表
- 尝试运用新知识
- 使用时间轴来记日期和事件
- 分析、解释数据
- 使用自己的推理和演绎技巧
- 创造并解决问题（和你的学习小组一起完成）
- 玩数学游戏（和你的学习小组一起完成）

'COMMITTING

EIGHT OR MORE INTELLIGENCES
VISUAL-SPATIAL INTELLIGENCE

- Used for visualisation and art

Characteristics:
- ☐ Thinks and remembers in pictures
- ☐ Good sense of imaging/use of mind's eye
- ☐ Sense of colour, good at art/ drawing
- ☐ Uses maps, charts and diagrams easily
- ☐ Sense of direction
- ☐ Good at driving/parking
- ☐ Well dressed

Art was a favourite subject at school.

Likes:
- ☐ Film and video
- ☐ Posters/pictures
- ☐ Drawing, painting, sculpting
- ☐ Doodling
- ☐ Colour
- ☐ Clothes, dressmaking
- ☐ Self assembly furniture/jigsaw puzzles and mazes
- ☐ Navigating
- ☐ Photography

Notes

_____

_____

_____

_____

_____

投入

八种或更多智能

视觉—空间智能

• 感受视觉空间，并把所感觉到的表现出来的能力

特点：

☐ 以图片的形式思考问题、记住
　 信息
☐ 富有想象力、善于想象
☐ 对颜色敏感，擅长美术、绘画
☐ 擅长使用地图、表格、图表
☐ 有方向感
☐ 善于驾驶、停车
☐ 穿着得体

喜欢：

☐ 电影、录像
☐ 海报、图片
☐ 绘画、油画、雕刻
☐ 涂鸦
☐ 色彩
☐ 衣服、缝纫
☐ 自组式家具、七巧板、
　 迷宫
☐ 导航
☐ 摄影

在学校时最喜欢美术。

COMMITTING

EIGHT OR MORE INTELLIGENCES
VISUAL-SPATIAL INTELLIGENCE

Learning techniques:
- Learn from film, video, slides, etc
- Use symbols, doodles, diagrams or, better still, mind map
- Design and produce a poster of the key facts and pin it up
- Highlight key points with different colours
- When you read, visualise events in your mind's eye; do not focus on the words
- Use heavily illustrated material to learn from
- Use visualisation to create a mental TV documentary with strong visual images
- Study in different places/areas of a room to gain a different perspective
- Convert information into diagrams or cartoons

Notes

_____

_____

_____

_____

_____

投入

八种或更多智能

视觉—空间智能

学习技巧：

- 从电影、录像、幻灯片中学习知识
- 使用符号、涂鸦、图表或最好是思维导图
- 设计制作一个关键信息海报并把它钉起来
- 用不同的颜色突出重点
- 一边阅读，一边在大脑中想象；不关注字本身
- 使用有大量插图的材料学习
- 在大脑中将信息展示成有强烈视觉图像的电视纪录片
- 在不同的地方、房间的不同区域学习以便获得不同的视角
- 把信息转化成图表或漫画

COMMITTING

EIGHT OR MORE INTELLIGENCES
MUSICAL INTELLIGENCE

- Used for rhythm, music and lyrics

Characteristics:
- ☐ Sensitive to pitch, rhythm and timbre
- ☐ Sensitive to emotion of music
- ☐ Changes mood with music
- ☐ Good at clapping in time to music
- ☐ Moves in time to music
- ☐ Remembers and repeats slogans and lyrics easily
- ☐ Theme music or jingles often pop into mind
- ☐ Good at selecting background music
- ☐ May be deeply spiritual

Music was a favourite subject at school.

Likes:
- ☐ Radio
- ☐ Concerts
- ☐ CD collection
- ☐ Making music – plays an instrument
- ☐ Singing – in a choir, group or alone
- ☐ Writing songs and/or music
- ☐ 'Working out' or relaxing to music

Notes

___

___

___

___

___

投入

八种或更多智能

音乐智能

• 感受节奏、音乐和歌词的能力

特点：

☐ 对音高、节奏、音色很敏感

☐ 对音乐的情感很敏感

☐ 心情会受到音乐的影响

☐ 善于随着音乐打拍子

☐ 会跟着音乐的调子舞动

☐ 很容易记住并重复标语和歌词

☐ 脑海中经常会响起主题曲和短曲

☐ 擅长选择背景音乐

☐ 追求精神生活

在学校时最喜欢音乐课。

喜欢：

☐ 收音机

☐ 音乐会

☐ CD 收藏

☐ 音乐创作——玩乐器

☐ 唱歌——合唱队、小组或是个人

☐ 写歌和（或）作曲

☐ 跟着音乐锻炼或是放松

COMMITTING

EIGHT OR MORE INTELLIGENCES
MUSICAL INTELLIGENCE

Learning techniques:

- Use music to relax before learning
- Study to music that represents what you are learning
- Study to baroque music (see page 176)
- Read rhythmically (use a metronome)
- Write a song, jingle, rap, poem, rhyme, etc, to summarise key points

Notes

_____

_____

_____

_____

_____

投入

八种或更多智能

音乐智能

学习技巧：

- 学习之前听音乐放松
- 一边学习，一边听跟所学内容有关的音乐
- 一边学习，一边听巴洛克音乐（参见 177 页）
- 有节奏地朗读（使用节拍器）
- 通过写歌、短曲、说唱、诗歌、韵律等来总结重点

COMMITTING

EIGHT OR MORE INTELLIGENCES
BODILY-KINAESTHETIC INTELLIGENCE →

- Used for touch and reflex

Characteristics:
- ☐ Never sits still
- ☐ Mechanically minded
- ☐ Likes to touch
- ☐ Solves problems physically hands on
- ☐ Good with their hands
- ☐ Controlled reflexes
- ☐ Control of body
- ☐ Control of objects
- ☐ Good timing

Likes:
- ☐ Sport/games
- ☐ Rough and tumble play/thrill rides at the fair
- ☐ Acting/drama
- ☐ Dancing
- ☐ Cooking/baking
- ☐ Handicrafts
- ☐ D.I.Y.
- ☐ Car maintenance

PE and handicraft lessons were favourite subjects at school.

Notes

投入

八种或更多智能

身体—动觉智能

• 触摸和反应的能力

特点：

☐ 无法安静地坐在某处
☐ 有搞机械的头脑
☐ 喜欢触摸
☐ 喜欢动手操作、解决问题
☐ 双手灵活
☐ 反射受控
☐ 控制身体
☐ 控制物体
☐ 善于把握时机

喜欢：

☐ 运动、游戏
☐ 混战，在游乐场玩惊险游乐
　　设施
☐ 表演、戏剧
☐ 跳舞
☐ 做饭、烘烤
☐ 手工
☐ 自己动手做
☐ 车辆保养

在学校时最喜欢体育和手工制作课。

COMMITTING

EIGHT OR MORE INTELLIGENCES
BODILY-KINAESTHETIC INTELLIGENCE

Learning techniques:

- Tackle learning *hands on*
- Learn from what you do
- Use roleplay/drama to act out what you are learning
- Get involved in the subject physically/use field trips
- Take action – write down key points or, better still, mind map
- Make models
- Write key points on to index cards and sort them into order/groups and/or pin them up in your study area
- Move about while you are learning
- Change activity often and take frequent breaks
- Mentally review your learning while jogging/swimming/walking, etc

Notes

_____

_____

_____

_____

_____

投入

八种或更多智能

身体—动觉智能

学习技巧：

- 亲自动手解决学习问题
- 从做的事情中学知识
- 用角色扮演、戏剧的形式展示你学的东西
- 亲身参与实地考察
- 采取行动——记下重点，或最好用思维导图
- 做模型
- 在索引卡上记下重点，并把它们排序或分组，也可以把索引卡钉在你学习的地方
- 学习时四处走动
- 经常变换活动，频繁休息
- 慢跑、游泳或走路时在大脑中复习所学内容

COMMITTING

EIGHT OR MORE INTELLIGENCES
INTERPERSONAL INTELLIGENCE

- Used for communicating with others

Characteristics:
- ☐ Relates to and mixes well with others
- ☐ Puts people at ease
- ☐ Has numerous friends
- ☐ Sympathetic to others' feelings
- ☐ Mediates between people in dispute
- ☐ Good communicator
- ☐ Good at negotiating
- ☐ Co-operative

Likes:
- ☐ Being with people
- ☐ Parties and social events
- ☐ Community activities
- ☐ Clubs
- ☐ Committee work
- ☐ Group activities/team tasks/games
- ☐ Managing/supervising
- ☐ Teaching/training
- ☐ Parenting

Notes

_____

_____

_____

_____

_____

投入

八种或更多智能

人际交流智能

· 与人交往的能力

特点:

- [ ] 善于与人交往，和人相处
  融洽
- [ ] 令人很舒服
- [ ] 朋友众多
- [ ] 同情别人的感受
- [ ] 协调他人的争端
- [ ] 善于交流
- [ ] 善于协商
- [ ] 有合作精神

喜欢:

- [ ] 与人相处
- [ ] 聚会、社交活动
- [ ] 社区活动
- [ ] 俱乐部
- [ ] 委员会工作
- [ ] 小组活动、团队任务、游戏
- [ ] 管理、监督
- [ ] 教学、培训
- [ ] 养育孩子

COMMITTING

EIGHT OR MORE INTELLIGENCES

INTERPERSONAL INTELLIGENCE

Learning techniques:

- Learn from others (form a learning set)
- Work in teams and learn together
- Talk to others to get and share answers
- Compare notes after a study session
- Make use of networking and mentoring
- Teach others
- Socialise during breaks
- Throw a party to celebrate/reward your success

Notes

投入

八种或更多智能

人际交流智能

学习技巧：

- 向别人学习（组成一个学习组）
- 团队作业、共同学习
- 与人交流，学习、分享答案
- 学习之后交换意见
- 利用网络和网络辅导
- 教别人
- 休息时与别人交流
- 举办庆功聚会

COMMITTING

EIGHT OR MORE INTELLIGENCES
INTRAPERSONAL INTELLIGENCE

- Used for self-discovery and self-analysis

Characteristics:
- ☐ Understands own feelings and behaviour
- ☐ Self-intuitive, knows own strengths
- ☐ Private
- ☐ Independent
- ☐ Wants to be different from the crowd
- ☐ Keeps a diary/journal
- ☐ Plans time effectively
- ☐ Is self-motivated
- ☐ Sets and achieves goals

Likes:
- ☐ Peace and quiet
- ☐ Daydreaming
- ☐ Reflecting/reminiscing
- ☐ Independence
- ☐ Achieving goals
- ☐ Own company
- ☐ Solitary pursuits
- ☐ Holidaying in a country cabin (not a busy hotel)
- ☐ Working for self (or has seriously contemplated it)

Notes

_____

_____

_____

_____

_____

投入

八种或更多智能

内省智能

• 自我发现和自我分析的能力

特点：

☐ 了解自己的感受和行为

☐ 自我直觉，了解自己的优势

☐ 文静内敛

☐ 独立

☐ 希望与众不同

☐ 坚持记日记或日志

☐ 有效安排时间

☐ 自我激励，有上进心

☐ 设立目标，实现目标

喜欢：

☐ 平和、安静

☐ 幻想·

☐ 反思、回忆

☐ 独立

☐ 实现目标

☐ 独处

☐ 独自追求目标

☐ 在乡村小屋度假（而不是嘈杂的酒店）

☐ 为自己工作（或者认真地沉思默想过这一点）

COMMITTING

EIGHT OR MORE INTELLIGENCES
INTRAPERSONAL INTELLIGENCE

Learning techniques:

- Use personal affirmations (see page 32)
- Set and achieve goals/targets with your learning
- Create personal interest, why the subject matters to you
- Get interested, involved and motivated with the arguments and main characters
- Take control of your learning
- Carry out independent study
- Seek out background information, especially the human interest angle
- Listen to your intuition
- Reflect, write or discuss what you experienced and how you felt
- Reflect on how the information fits in with your existing knowledge and experiences

Notes

_____

_____

_____

_____

_____

投入

八种或更多智能

内省智能

学习技巧：

- 自我肯定（参见 33 页）

- 设立并实现学习的目标

- 培养自己的兴趣，为什么这个科目对你很重要

- 对辩论和主要角色感兴趣，并积极参与

- 掌控自己的学习

- 独立学习

- 寻求背景知识，尤其是人类兴趣方面

- 听从自己的直觉

- 反思、写下或者讨论你的经历和感想

- 思考一下新信息是如何融入你的已知知识和经历的

COMMITTING

EIGHT OR MORE INTELLIGENCES
NATURALISTIC INTELLIGENCE

Characteristics:
- ☐ Attuned to the natural world
- ☐ Good at identifying and classifying
- ☐ Can remember habitats of plants and animals
- ☐ Comfortable in different types of environments
- ☐ Troubled by pollution
- ☐ Keen sensory skills – sight, sound, smell, touch, taste

Likes:
- ☐ The outdoors
- ☐ Camping, hiking or gardening, etc
- ☐ Being close to wild animals and plants
- ☐ Observing and identifying wildlife
- ☐ Exploring and expeditions
- ☐ Taking care of living things
- ☐ Collections, scrapbooks or logs
- ☐ TV programmes, books and videos about the natural world
- ☐ Astronomy, evolution and the environment

Science was a favourite subject at school.

Notes

投入

八种或更多智能

自然探索智能

特点：

- ☐ 适应自然世界
- ☐ 善于识别、分类
- ☐ 能够记住动植物的栖息地
- ☐ 适应各种环境
- ☐ 对污染反感
- ☐ 灵敏的感官——视觉、听觉、嗅觉、触觉、味觉

喜欢：

- ☐ 户外活动
- ☐ 野营、徒步旅行或园艺等
- ☐ 亲近野生动植物
- ☐ 观察、辨别野生生物
- ☐ 喜欢探索、探险
- ☐ 照顾有生命的物体
- ☐ 收集、剪贴簿、日志
- ☐ 关于自然世界的电视节目、书籍和录像
- ☐ 天文学、演变进化、环境

在学校时最喜欢科学。

COMMITTING

EIGHT OR MORE INTELLIGENCES
NATURALISTIC INTELLIGENCE

Learning techniques:

- Learn outdoors, eg on field trips and practical work
- Use tools for investigating, eg magnifying glass, microscope and binoculars
- Collect and organise data from observations
- Sort things and place them in hierarchies
- Look for patterns, similarities, make connections
- Classify, discriminate or look for differences
- Stimulate your senses, eg use accelerated learning toys to stimulate your sense of touch as you learn, use scented pens and music
- Have plants and fish where you learn
- Get plenty of fresh air and even learn outdoors

Notes

投入

八种或更多智能

自然探索智能

学习技巧：

- 户外学习，比如实地考察、实际操作
- 使用调查工具，比如放大镜、显微镜和双筒望远镜
- 收集、整理观察数据
- 把东西分类，并按等级存放
- 寻找模式、相同点，建立联系
- 分类、区分或寻找不同点
- 刺激你的感官，比如学习时使用加速学习玩具来刺激你的触觉，使用香味笔，听音乐
- 在学习的地方摆放植物和鱼
- 获得足够的新鲜空气，甚至在户外学习

COMMITTING

POWER READING

PREPARATION

- Start with introductory text such as an encyclopedia or children's book
- Find the three best books in your area of interest (ask for referrals)
- List key headings of existing knowledge or mind map it
- Define your questions – the six W's (see page 62) so you read with a sense of interest
- Browse through each book casually and rapidly to identify:
  - organisation and structure   – appendices   – contents, etc
  - diagrams/pictures   – preface
- Be selective, do not go further if it does not add to your existing knowledge
- Organise your reading into chunks (salami method)
- When you take breaks:
  - cup and uncup your hands over your eyes
  - focus on distant objects
  - do not rub your eyes

Notes

_____

_____

_____

_____

_____

投入

促进阅读

准备

- 从阅读介绍性文本开始，比如百科全书或者儿童书籍
- 找到自己感兴趣的领域中三本最好的书（找别人推荐）
- 列出已有知识的关键标题或者做思维导图
- 定义你的问题，借鉴六个W（参见63页），这样你就会带着兴趣去阅读
- 随意快速地浏览每一本书以辨别：
  - ——组织和结构　　　　——附录　　　　　　——内容
  - ——图表、图片　　　　——前言
- 有选择性；如果对你没有帮助，就不必深读
- 把阅读划分为一个个板块（意大利腊肠法）
- 休息时：
  - ——重复把手窝成杯状放在眼前、再放下来的动作
  - ——聚焦远处的物体
  - ——不要揉眼睛

COMMITTING

POWER READING
HOW TO READ

- Scan read for ideas and principles, not individual words
- Read the text; concentrate on beginning and end of paragraphs and chapters, or wherever else you identify key ideas are communicated
- Mark pages, highlight, underline, make notes, use codes as you go
- Skip over difficult text, return to it later when you have the full picture
- Read difficult text aloud
- Make key notes or mind map at the end of each chapter
- Review your notes/mind map
- Summarise the whole book in a few key notes/master mind map

TIPS
- Do not be afraid to disregard the book at any stage
- Never feel obliged to read a book cover to cover: only read what you want
- Be flexible; adapt your reading to the style of the material

Remember to celebrate your success and reward yourself.

Notes

投入

促进阅读

如何阅读

- 浏览文本，查找观点、原则，而不是个别的词语
- 阅读文本；关注段落和章节的首尾，或者是任何你发现重点信息的地方
- 标出页码，突出强调，划下划线，做笔记，不读时做上标记
- 跳过难读的文本，等了解了整体大意后再回过头阅读
- 大声朗读难理解的文本
- 读完每章之后都做重点笔记或是思维导图
- 复习笔记／思维导图
- 用几个重点笔记总结全书／掌握思维导图

小贴士：

- 任何阶段都不要害怕忽视了书
- 不要觉得必须把一本书从头读到尾：只读那些你想知道的内容就可以了
- 灵活一点；阅读时，要适应文本的风格

记得庆祝自己的成功并且奖励自己。

COMMITTING

POWER READING

Try this simple test – answer all questions:

1 What is your favourite book?
2 Which spelling is correct: feasabality or feasibility?
3 What was your favourite subject at school?
4 Work out what X is: $2 \times X + 3 = 15$
5 What did you have for breakfast?
6 Write your name backwards
7 What is your favourite film?
8 Repeat question 5
9 Ignore all the questions. If you answered, then see 10 below, if not turn the page
10 Re-read **Power Reading**: time spent now may save time in the future

Notes

_____

_____

_____

_____

_____

投入

促进阅读

试试这个简单的测试——回答所有的问题：

1. 你最喜欢的书是什么？

2. 哪个拼写是对的：feasabality 还是 feasibility？

3. 你在学校最喜欢的科目是什么？

4. 如果 $2 \times X + 3 = 15$，求出 X 是多少？

5. 你早餐吃什么？

6. 从后往前写你的名字。

7. 你最喜欢的电影是哪一部？

8. 重复问题 5。

9. 忽略所有的问题。如果你已经回答了，那么看一下第 10 条。如果没有的话，请直接翻页。

10. 再读一遍**促进阅读**：

　　磨刀不误砍柴工。

COMMITTING

LEARNING SET
BENEFITS

Try getting together with a group to learn. The ideal number is two to six people.

- Makes learning enjoyable
- You give each other mutual support
- Saves time, as you will not have to research the whole subject
- Mixing learning styles ensures better learning
- Gain different opinions and viewpoints
- Raises the quality of your work
- You are committed if you are participating and contributing
- You will also learn how to work as a group, communicate and present your ideas
- Learning is improved – two heads are better than one

 *Notes*

投入

学习小组

好处

试着和小组一起学习，最佳人数是 2 到 6 人。

- 让学习变得有趣
- 相互帮助、支持
- 节约时间，因为你不必研究整个课题
- 混合的学习模式保证了更好的学习效果
- 收获不同的意见和观点
- 提高工作质量
- 如果你参与了并且做出了贡献，你就会愿意做出最大的努力
- 你也将会学到怎样以小组的方式工作，怎样与人交流，展现自己的观点
- 学习效果会得到改善——人多智广

COMMITTING

LEARNING SET

Reasoning
- Establish a working contract for learning together
- Define the common objective and goal

Planning
- Break the learning into sections and assign to the set members
- Complete a learning plan

Committing
- Support each other, share opinions, experiences, knowledge and fears
- Use individuals' strengths, especially learning styles

Reflecting
- Present your section to the set, proves if you know the subject
- Review how the set worked, to improve for the future
- Keep the set together for future learning projects
- Compete with other learning sets

 *Notes*

_____

_____

_____

_____

_____

投入

学习小组

推理
- 制定一个一起学习的约定
- 规定共同的目标和追求

计划
- 把学习划分为一个个板块，再分配给每个成员
- 完成一个学习计划

承诺
- 相互支持，交流意见、经历、知识和担忧
- 发挥个人的优势，尤其是学习方式

反思
- 向小组展示你的部分，证明你是否知道这个主题
- 回顾小组工作开展得如何，积极改进，为未来做准备
- 小组保持联系，将来有学习项目时再一起合作
- 和其他的学习小组竞争

COMMITTING

ON COURSE TECHNIQUES

Preparation	• Complete any required pre-course study
	• If there is none, gain a basic understanding of the subject

Questions	• Prepare questions, know what you want to achieve
	• Use the six W's

Seating	• Front and centre; you are more involved and can more easily focus on the trainer
	• From this position visual aids are easier to see, speech is easier to hear
	• Watch your posture; sit upright and attentive

Trainer	• Concentrate on the message not the messenger: ignore any irritating mannerisms
	• If you have done your preparation and prepared questions this will be easier

Listen	• Imagine the trainer is talking to you personally
	• Do not read notes or ask colleagues to explain during a training session
	• If you have missed a point ask the trainer

Notes

_____

_____

_____

_____

_____

投入

课程技巧

准备
- 完成要求的课前学习
- 如果没有的话，搜索信息，对课题有个基本的了解

问题
- 准备问题，知道自己想要获得什么
- 使用"六个 W"

座位
- 坐在前排和中间；你能更加积极参与，把精力集中在培训师身上
- 在这样的位置，你更容易看见视觉教具，更容易听到讲课
- 注意你的姿势；坐直，专心听讲

培训师
- 关注信息本身而不是传递信息的人；忽视任何惹人不快的言谈举止
- 如果你已经做好了准备，而且准备了问题，那一切就容易多了

倾听
- 想象培训师是在和你单独交流
- 培训过程中，不要读笔记或是请同事帮你解释问题
- 错过重点时及时提问

COMMITTING

ON COURSE TECHNIQUES

Notes	• Mind map the key points; this will free up your time to listen
Learning	• Use your own personal learning style • If this is not possible during a learning session, you have some post-course work to do
Breaks	• If you can, go outside for fresh air and a walk. Remember how daylight affects your alertness (page 50) • Drink water, not tea or coffee (the brain is 70% water) • Do not discuss what you are learning (let your subconscious process it) • Have a light lunch and give your body time to digest it before re-entering the training room
Colleagues	• At the end of day or course share your learning: you will be surprised at what you have missed and gain a different perspective
Review/ Consolidate	• At the end of the day or course review your learning • Follow up action points and keep your learning current and fresh

Notes

_____

_____

_____

_____

_____

投入

课程技巧

笔记
- 把重点做成思维导图：这将节约你的时间，让你能专心听课

学习
- 采用自己的学习方式
- 如果一节课中你做不到采用自己的学习方式的话，你将会有一些课下任务要做

休息
- 可以的话，去外面呼吸一下新鲜空气，散散步。日光会影响你的灵敏度（参见 51 页）
- 多喝水，而不是茶或咖啡（大脑 70% 是由水组成的）
- 不要讨论你学习的内容（让你的潜意识自行加工处理）
- 午餐吃得清淡点。不要急着进入教室，留出时间让你的身体消化

同事
- 一天结束或是课程结束时，和其他人交流分享：你会惊讶地发现自己遗漏了很多内容，并且能收获不同的观点

复习、巩固
- 一天结束或是课程结束时，复习所学内容
- 跟进行动重点，保证你的学习与时俱进

LEARNING TRANSFER GRID

Fortune magazine undertook research with the 500 highest performing companies in the USA, asking about training. From the answers they created this grid, which reflects which areas contribute most significantly to the success of those companies. The research identified the most important elements of training in terms of enabling delegates to change their behaviour permanently, incorporating new skills into their working practices.

The best course in the world will be useless unless some part of the content is put into practice afterwards. Conversely, act on a single new skill/piece of information learned from a poor course, and you will have developed and become more effective.

An ongoing programme of post-course activity is vital to ensure that you gain optimum benefit from your attendance.

Input from	Before training	During training	After training
Supervisor	3	8	2
Delegate	6	4	1
Trainer	7	5	9

1 = The area where the greatest emphasis needs to be, to ensure positive benefits from training.

9 = The area where the least emphasis needs to be, to ensure positive benefits from training.

Notes

_____

_____

_____

_____

_____

投入

学习迁移表格

《财富》杂志就培训方面调查了美国业绩最出色的前 500 名公司。它们根据公司的回答做了这个表格，反映了哪些方面对这些公司的成功贡献最大。调查发现，培训最重要的要素就是能让受训者永久地改变行为，以及将新技巧运用到工作实践中。

如果课程的内容没有被用于实践的话，那么即使是世界上最好的课程也没有用。相反，即使是运用了一门差强人意的课程中的某个新技巧或某条信息，也会提高你的工作效率。

课后活动的持续项目对确保你从课程中获得最大收益是很重要的。

输入来自	培训前	培训中	培训后
监督人	3	8	2
代表学员	6	4	1
培训师	7	5	9

1= 为确保培训收到积极效果最需要关注的地方。

9= 为确保培训收到积极效果最不需要关注的地方。

COMMITTING

MEMORY
WHAT IS MEMORY?

Memory consists of three stages:

Registration • You get information

Retention • You file information, which has the **potential** to be retrieved

Retrieval • You find the information at some later stage when you need it

Retrieval consists of:

– Recall: voluntarily or involuntarily return the information to consciousness

– Recognition: you cannot recall the information but you recognise it when you see it

'Retention' is not the problem, 'retrieval' is.

Notes

投入

记忆

记忆是什么？

记忆由三个阶段组成：

登录　　· 获得信息

保留　　· 将信息归档，**可能**会重新提取信息

提取　　· 之后当你需要的时候，找到这个信息

提取包括：

——回忆：自觉地或是不自觉地想起这个信息

——辨识：你不记得这个信息，但当你再看见
　　　　它时，你会立刻辨识出它

问题不在于"保留"，而在于"提取"。

COMMITTING

MEMORY
RETENTION

You file information, which has the **potential to be retrieved**:

Hypnosis	• Under hypnosis people have recalled *forgotten* memories perfectly
Near death experiences	• *My whole life flashed before my eyes* • Emotion is closely linked to memory • Highly emotive events are memorable and also stimulate old memories
Surprise random recall	• *Déja vu* • Stimulation of the senses can bring about recall of *forgotten* memories • A certain smell or taste brings it all back
Dreams	• Vivid dreams recalling *forgotten* memories and events

Turn the page and write down everything you can remember from this page. When you turn back to this page to check, the fact that you recognise it means you have **retention**. The problem is **retrieval**.

You have experienced **recognition** and involuntary **recall**. The trick is to master **voluntary recall**.

Notes

投入

记忆

保留

你将信息归档，以后可能会**重新提取信息**：

催眠状态	• 催眠状态下人们会完整地记起已经忘掉的记忆
濒死体验	• 一生都浮现在眼前
	• 感情与记忆紧密相联
	• 高情绪化的事情容易记住，而且会激起以前的回忆
不经意的惊喜回忆	• 似曾相识
	• 对感官的刺激，让你想起忘却的记忆
	• 某种香气或味道让记忆全部都回来了
梦	• 生动的梦境使人回忆起过去的事情

翻到下一页，写下本页中你记得的所有信息。当你再翻到这一页做检查时，如果你认得出这些信息，就表示你有**"保留"**。

问题是**"提取"**。

你已经体验了**"识别"**和**"不自觉回忆"**。

技巧是掌握**自觉回忆**。

COMMITTING

MEMORY

HOW IT WORKS

There are three types of memory:

Immediate (sensory) memory – seconds
Limited capacity – seven inputs at once is the average person's limit.
This is where input is held until you select what you wish to work with.

Short-term memory – hours or days
This is where you react to new inputs that the immediate memory
has selected to work with. Like the immediate memory, this easily
reaches overload. To get information into the long-term memory
requires repetition of the input in a variety of ways.
(See **Learning Styles** and **Multiple Intelligences.**)

Long-term memory – months or years
This is where you make sense of what you are learning,
linking and comparing it to existing learning. The new learning
helps shape existing learning, and is then applied.

Notes

_____

_____

_____

_____

_____

投入

记忆

它是如何工作的?

有三种记忆:

瞬时记忆（感觉记忆）——秒

有限容量——一般人的极限是一次输入七个信息。在你做出决定选择什么信息之前，输入的信息都被存储在这儿。

短时记忆——小时或天

瞬时记忆选择的信息在这儿得到了短暂保持。和瞬时记忆一样，短时记忆也很容易超载。通过各种方法不断重复该信息才能把它转化成长时记忆。（参见**"学习方式"**和**"多元智能"**部分）

长时记忆——月或年

你理解了正在学习的内容，把它们和已有的知识联系起来或是比较一下。新学的知识融入已有的知识，再被运用。

COMMITTING

MEMORY

SENSORY MEMORY TO LONG-TERM MEMORY

- Learning involves getting information from sensory memory into the long-term memory
- Anything in sensory memory can get in to the long-term memory through **learning**
- Long-term memory has no known storage limit
- When people talk about *memory* they usually mean **retrieval** from long-term memory

Notes

_____

_____

_____

_____

_____

投入

记忆

感觉记忆到长时记忆

- 学习包括把感觉记忆转化成长时记忆
- 通过**学习**，任何感觉记忆都可以被转化成长时记忆
- 长时记忆没有已知的容量限制
- 当人们说起记忆时，他们通常指的是从长时记忆中**提取**

COMMITTING

MEMORY

TEST

Read the following list of words, slowly, once. Then cover them up and answer the questions that follow.

HAND
CASE
ME
CAR
BOOK
AND
BRAIN
ME
HERE
TREE
MISSISSIPPI
OF
DOOR
AND
MUSIC
ME
HOME
FILM
WHITE
AND

Notes

投入

记忆

测试

　　一次慢慢读完下面的词汇。之后把它们盖起来，回答接下来的
问题。

```
                            密
                            西
      案        大  这  西        音      电 白
   手 例 我 车 书 和 脑 我 儿 树 比 的 门 和 乐 我 家 影 色 和
```

COMMITTING

MEMORY

TEST

How many of the first five words can you recall?

....

How many of the last five words can you recall?

....

Can you recall any words that appeared more than once?

....

Was there any word that was outstandingly different from the rest?

....

How many words can you recall that have something to do with what you have already read?

....

How many of the words from the middle of the list, that you have not already noted above, can you recall?

....

Read on to check your results.

 *Notes*

_____

_____

_____

_____

_____

投入

记忆

测试

前五个词你记得几个？

最后五个词你记得几个？

你记得出现过不止一次的词吗？

有和其他词显著不同的词吗？

你记得多少个和你之前阅读的内容有关的词？

除了前面提到过的，处在中间位置的词你还记得多少？

接着往下读，检查你的成绩。

COMMITTING

MEMORY
LEARNING WITHOUT BREAKS

Primacy: The start of a learning session is more memorable than the middle

First events are more memorable

In the memory test you will have more easily recalled some first words

Recency: The end of a learning session is more memorable than the middle

Recent events are more memorable

In the memory test you will have more easily recalled some last words

Notes

_____

_____

_____

_____

_____

投入

记忆

不休息地学习

首因效应：学习刚开始时会比学习中途更容易记住信息

开始的事情更容易记住

在记忆测试中，你更容易记住一些前面的词

近因效应：学习快结束时会比学习中途更容易记住信息

最近的事情更容易记住

在记忆测试中，你更容易记住一些最后的词

COMMITTING

MEMORY
LEARNING WITHOUT BREAKS

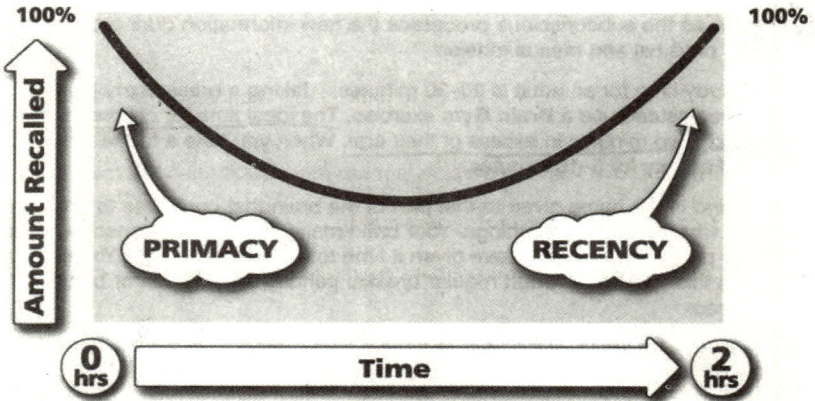

投入

记忆

不休息地学习

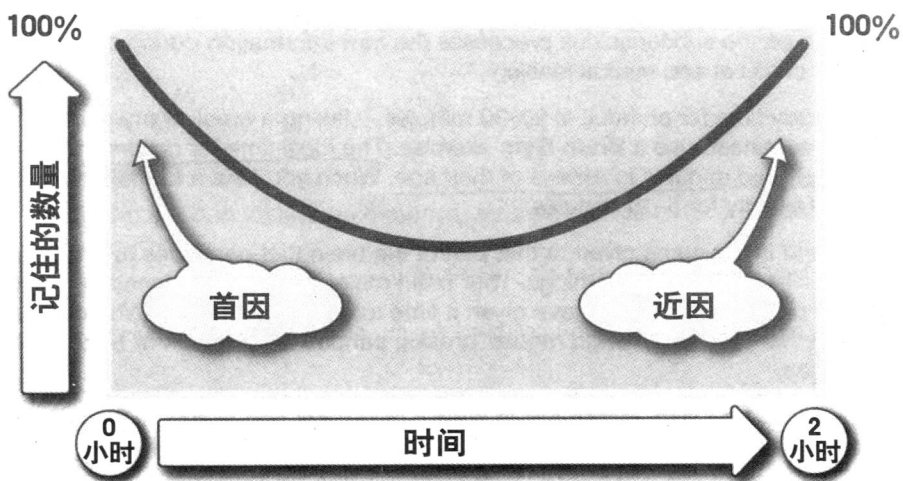

COMMITTING

MEMORY

LEARNING WITH REGULAR BREAKS

- Keeps recall high, due to the increased effects of primacy and recency
- Increases as the subconscious processes the new information during breaks
- Relieves physical and mental tension

The ideal study time for an adult is 20–30 minutes.   Taking a break every half-hour may be disruptive. Instead use a **Brain Gym** exercise. The ideal time for children to study is approximately two minutes in excess of their age. When you take a formal break, perform a change of activity for 5–10 minutes.

The slow mind is the name given to that part of the brain that continues to process information while you do other things. Your brain makes important connections and finds solutions to problems after you have given it time to digest information. You can help benefit from this process through regular breaks, periods of reflection or by using brain gym exercises.

When you break for lunch, remember to have a light meal and give your body time to digest it before re-starting your learning.

Notes

_____

_____

_____

_____

_____

记忆

有正常休息的学习

- 随着首因、近因效应的增强，回忆也增强
- 休息时随着潜意识加工处理信息，记忆也随之增强
- 缓解身体和精神的紧张

成人的理想学习时间是 20 ～ 30 分钟，但是每半小时休息一次是不利于学习效果的。你可以代之以**脑力健身操**。儿童的理想学习时间大约是他们的年龄再加 2 分钟。正规休息时，活动 5 ～ 10 分钟。

慢速大脑指的是当你做其他事情时仍然继续加工信息的大脑部分。大脑获得足够的时间消化信息后，它就会建立重要的联系并找到解决问题的办法。有规律的休息、反思、脑力健身操都能使你获益良多。

午餐时吃得清淡一点。不要急着学习，留出时间让食物在体内消化。

COMMITTING

MEMORY
LEARNING WITH REGULAR BREAKS

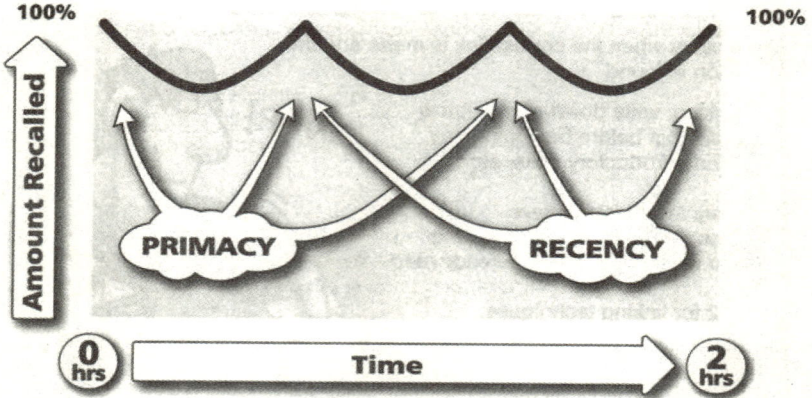

100%   100%

Amount Recalled

PRIMACY   RECENCY

0 hrs   Time   2 hrs

Notes

_____

_____

_____

_____

_____

投入

记忆

有正常休息的学习

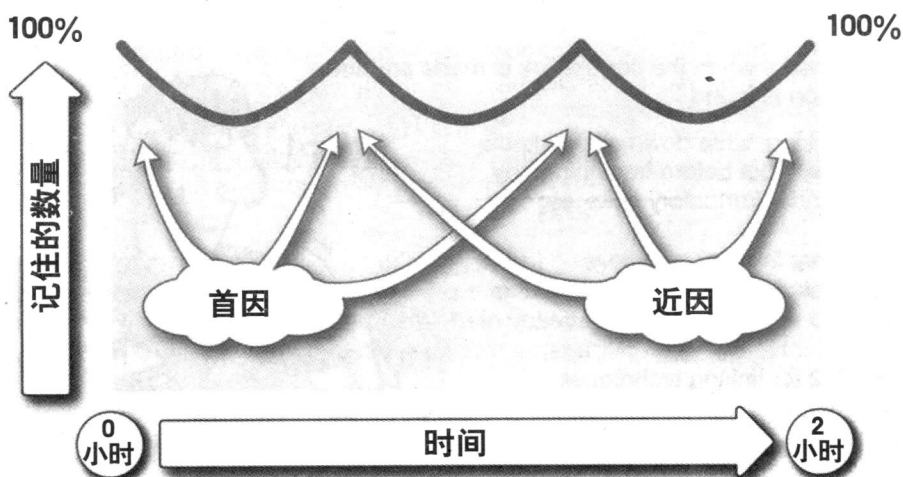

COMMITTING

MEMORY
THE EFFECT OF LINKING

- You learn by linking new information to existing knowledge
- Recall occurs when the correct link is made and the information is found
- To aid linking, write down all you know about a subject before beginning any study, read introductory texts, etc

In the memory test you may have recalled book, brain *and/or* music *as the words link to what you will have already read.*

See page 174 for linking techniques.

SNAP!

Notes

_____

_____

_____

_____

_____

投入

记忆

联系的效果

- 把新信息和已有知识联系起来学习
- 当建立起正确的联系时，就可能出现回忆并且找到信息
- 为了帮助联系，学习之前，先写下你知道的关于该课题的所有内容，阅读介绍性文本，等等

记忆测试中，你可能会回忆起书、大脑和（或）音乐这三个词，因为它们可能和你之前读到的内容有联系。

参见 175 页学习联系的技巧。

啪!

COMMITTING

MEMORY
THE EFFECT OF LINKING

Notes

_____

_____

_____

_____

_____

投入

记忆

联系的效果

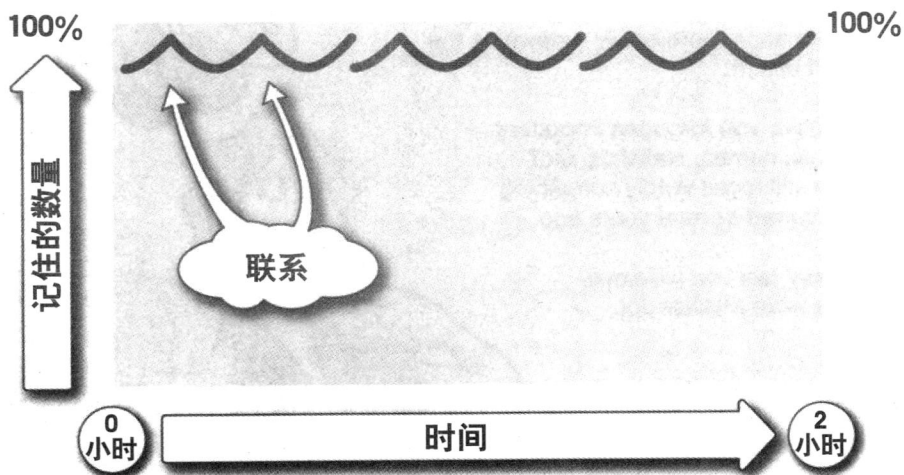

COMMITTING

MEMORY
THE EFFECT OF OUTSTANDINGNESS

You will recall unusual, outstanding, strange or absurd information more easily (known as the Von Restorff effect).

How often have you forgotten important appointments, names, statistics, etc? Yet you can still recall vividly something silly that occurred several years ago.

In the memory test you will have recalled the word Mississippi.

 *Notes*

投入

记忆

突出效应

你更容易回忆起不寻常的、突出的、奇怪的或是荒诞的信息（即冯·雷斯托夫效应）。

你是否经常会忘记重要的约会、名字、统计数据等？然而你却依然能清晰地记得若干年前发生的糗事。

记忆测试中，你可能会记住"密西西比"这个词。

COMMITTING

MEMORY
THE EFFECT OF OUTSTANDINGNESS

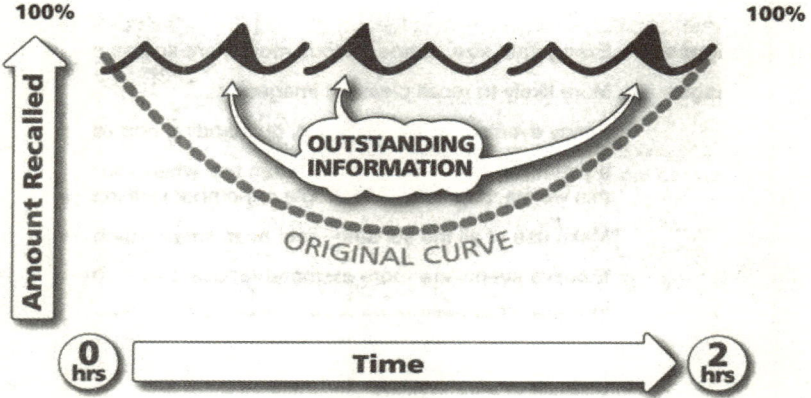

100%   100%

Amount Recalled

OUTSTANDING INFORMATION

ORIGINAL CURVE

0 hrs   **Time** →   **2** hrs

Notes

_____

_____

_____

_____

_____

投入

记忆

突出效应

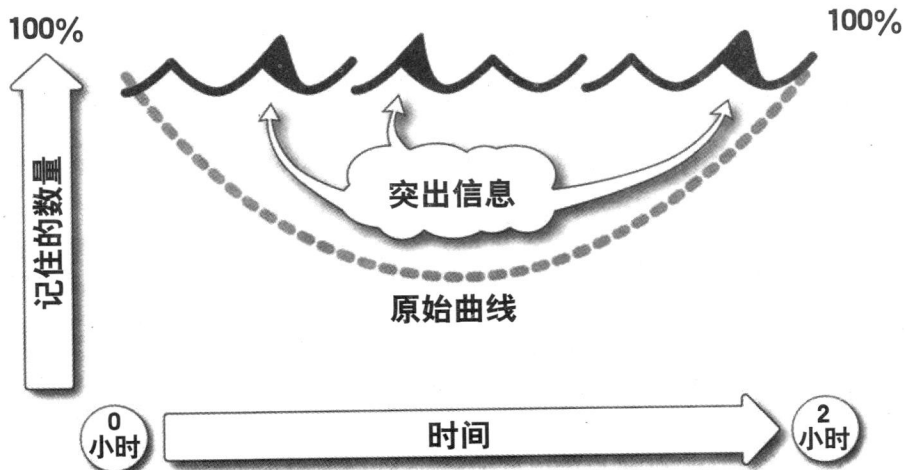

COMMITTING

MEMORY

LINKING

Link information effectively and creatively by using:

Outstandingness Exaggerate size, shape, colour, movement and all of the following

Positive images More likely to recall pleasant images

Humour Funny events are more positive, outstanding and easier to recall

Sexuality If you remember one of these seven tips when you turn the page, this will be the one; most people remember well in this area

Sensuality Make use of all the senses – see, hear, smell, touch and taste

Emotion Emotive events are more memorable: use love, hate, fear, etc

Personality There is no substitute for your own images and links; you are more likely to remember what you created
Personal events and experiences are more memorable; involve yourself in your images

Notes

投入

记忆

联系

通过使用以下要素有效地、创造性地联系信息：

突出性　　夸大尺寸、形状、颜色、动作以及下面所有的要素

积极形象　更可能回忆起令人愉快的形象

幽默　　　有趣的事情更突出，更与众不同，因此更容易被
　　　　　　记住

性　　　　如果翻页时你只能记住本页七个要素中的一个的
　　　　　　话，那么一定就是"性"。大多数人对这方面的事
　　　　　　情都记得很牢

感官　　　使用所有的感官——视觉、听觉、嗅觉、触觉、
　　　　　　味觉

情感　　　情绪化的事情更容易记住：使用爱、恨、恐惧等

个性　　　你自己的形象和联系是无可替代的；你更容易记
　　　　　　住自己创造的东西
　　　　　　个人事件和经历更容易记住；参与自己的形象建设

COMMITTING

MUSIC

Certain types of music can match the body's rhythms, heartbeat, brain waves, etc, inducing a state of relaxed alertness, for learning. Dr Georgi Lozanov identified that baroque music, in particular, leaves the mind relaxed and open to learning.

- Classical pieces (1750–1825) and romantic pieces (1820–1900) work best when you are learning new information.

- Baroque pieces (1600–1750) work best when you are reviewing information.
  The 60-70 beats per minute (the same as the earth's rotation) also induce alpha brain waves (see Brain Waves, page 6)

Experiment with different types of music, to see what works best for you. If you find it distracting – don't use it.

Notes

投入

音乐

　　某些类型的音乐可以和人体的节奏、心跳、脑电波等相配合，导致一种放松的、灵敏的学习状态。乔治·洛扎诺夫博士发现巴洛克音乐尤其能使大脑放松，促进学习。

　　• 学习新知识时，听古典音乐（1750–1825）和浪漫音乐（1820–1900）效果最佳。

　　• 复习知识时，听巴洛克音乐（1600–1750）效果最佳。
　　每秒 60 至 70 拍（和地球的自转一样）也能够激发大脑的阿尔法波（参见第 7 页脑电波部分）。

　　拿不同类型的音乐来做实验，看看哪一种对你效果最好。如果你觉得音乐使你分心的话，就不要听了。

COMMITTING

MIND MAPS

BENEFITS

Mirrors how the brain looks and works

Stimulates both right and left hemispheres of the brain

Makes use of linking

Makes use of different learning styles

Makes use of different intelligences $\sqrt{8^2}$

Visual excitement aids memory

Your ideas are easier to recall

Saves time, only recording and reviewing key words

Easy to review, recreate from memory and check against original

Numerous other uses eg making a presentation, project planning, writing reports, creativity and brainstorming sessions, taking minutes

The Mind Map® created and designed by Tony Buzan. Learner's Pocketbook Mind Mapping officially approved by Tony Buzan.

Notes

投入

思维导图

优势

模仿大脑的样子
和工作机制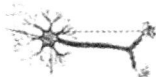

更容易记起你
自己的想法

刺激左右两个脑半球

节约时间，只记录、复习
重点词语

使用联系

容易复习，回忆并检测

使用不同的学习方式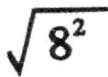

有很多其他的用途，比如
做报告, 项目规划, 写报告,

使用不同的智能 $\sqrt{8^2}$

举行有关创造力和头脑风
暴的会议，做会议记录

视觉刺激辅助记忆

思维导图[®]是由托尼·布赞设计创造的。《做个学习者》中的思
维导图部分是经过他正式同意使用的。

COMMITTING

MIND MAP MAXIMS

Paper

Good quality to stimulate all the senses
Blank – nothing to confine your creativity
Landscape – maximum space
Only use one side – easier to read

Central Image

Has more associations than a word and aids memory
Central image attracts the eye
Size 5 x 5 cm (2" x 2"), open no frame
Use at least four colours, appealing – encourages learning

If you must use a word, use **DIMENSION** and colour

Notes

_____

_____

_____

_____

_____

思维导图准则

纸

质量好以刺激所有的感官
空白——没有东西能限制你的创造力
全景——最大空间
只使用一边——更方便阅读

中央形象

比一个单词有更多的联系，并能辅助记忆
中央形象吸引眼球
大小 5×5 厘米（2"×2"），无框
使用至少四种颜色，吸引眼球——鼓励学习

如果必须要用一个词的话，用**维度**和颜色

COMMITTING

MIND MAP MAXIMS

Branches

Main branches thicker, symbolise importance
Curved lines – stimulate visual interest
Length of line = length of word

STIMULATE

one word per line

Words

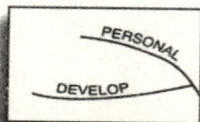

Only record key words
PRINT WORDS ON LINE
Main branch word – UPPER CASE
Secondary branches – lower case
Vary size relative to IMPORTANCE
Use for **EMPHASIS** **STRESS**

Notes

_____

_____

_____

_____

_____

投入

思维导图准则

分支

主干粗一点，象征重要性
曲线——刺激视觉兴趣
线的长度 = 单词的长度

刺激

单词

只记录关键单词

每条线上一个单词

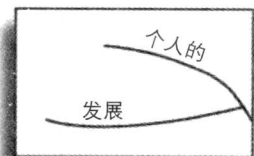

把单词用印刷体写在线上
主干词语——大写
第二分支——小写

根据**重要性**决定词语的大小

用来

强调   着重

MIND MAP MAXIMS

Images

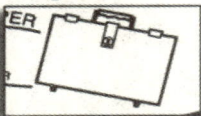

Stimulate the right brain – aid memory
Have more associations than words
Attract the eye, encourage learning
Eye takes in images faster than words
Where possible replace words with pictures

Colour

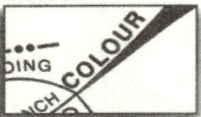

Stimulates the right brain – aids memory
Use increases short-term memory by 75% and
long-term by 25%
Use one colour per main branch theme
Use for coding, enables faster access to information

Codes

Use codes for instant linking of information, recurring
themes and/or to save time ⚬ ✔ ✘ ✚ ✿ ▲ ✳ ●
Use arrows to guide the eye to connecting themes
→ ↔ ↘ ↗ ➘ → ➠ ➡ ➢ ➤ ➧ ➹ ➽ ⇔ ⇨

Notes

_____

_____

_____

_____

_____

投入

思维导图准则

图像

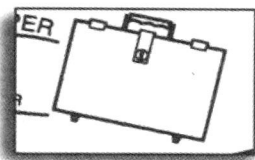

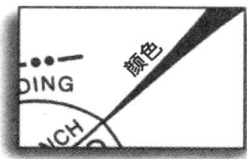

刺激右脑——辅助记忆

比单词有更多的联系

吸引眼球，鼓励学习

比起单词，眼睛能更快地接收图像

可能的话，用图片代替单词

颜色

刺激右脑——辅助记忆

把短期记忆提高 75％，长期记忆提高 25％

每个主干主题使用一种颜色

用于编码，能更快接收信息

代码

使用代码即时联系信息、重复出现的主题、并且（或者）节约时间 ➼ ✔ ✘ ✚ ✿ ▲ ✳ ●

使用箭头提示眼睛注意有联系的主题

➔ ↔ ➷ ↗ ➤ ➔ ➡ ➡ ➢ ➤ ➧ ↗ ➼ ↩ ➩

MIND MAP MAXIMS

Spacing

Leave space
for CLARITY and ADD + ITIONS

Personal style

Learning style is personal
Personal events are more memorable
Develop a personal style for your mind maps

Have fun

When learning is fun you learn faster and recall more
You are more likely to repeat the experience
It takes 72 muscles to frown and only
14 to smile

Relax and
enjoy learning

Notes

_____

_____

_____

_____

_____

投入

思维导图准则

间距

留出空间
清晰明了，方便补充

个人风格

学习方式因人而异
自己的事情更容易记住
为你的思维导图建立起一种个人风格

玩得开心

当学习是种乐趣的时候，你就能学得更快，
记得更多
你很可能会重复这个经历
皱眉需要牵动 72 块肌肉，微笑却只要 14 块

放松，
享受学习

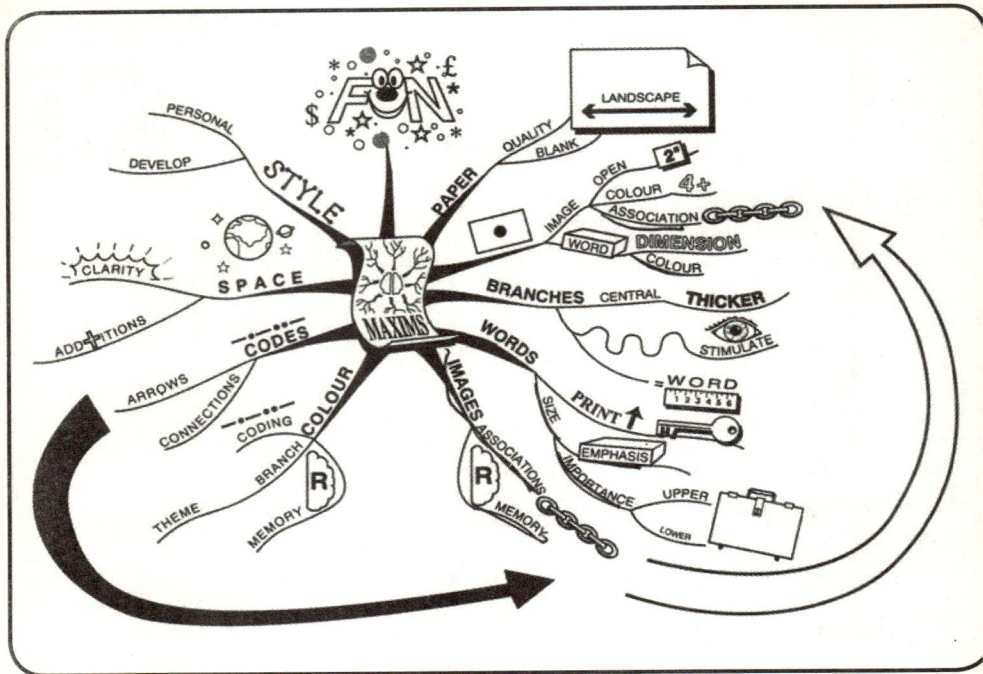

![Notes]

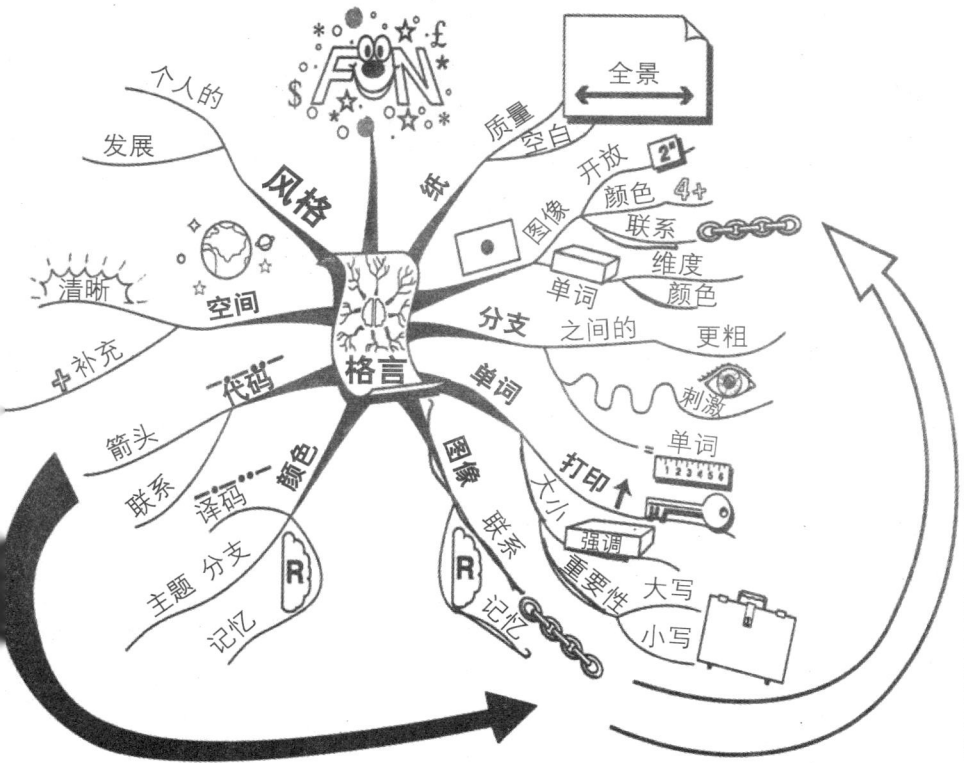

REVIEW

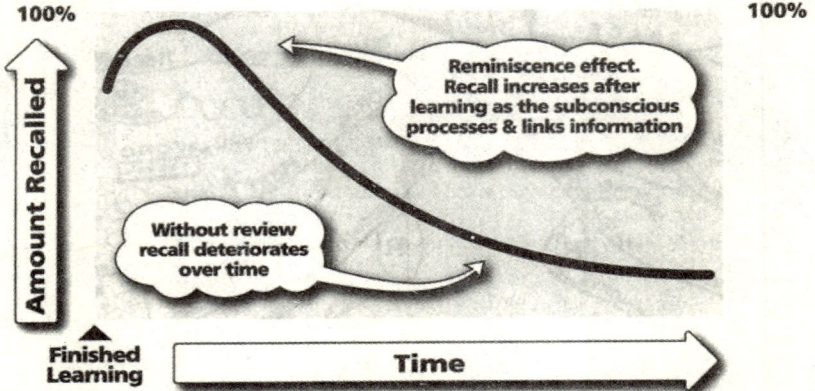

100% — Amount Recalled — 100%

Reminiscence effect. Recall increases after learning as the subconscious processes & links information

Without review recall deteriorates over time

Finished Learning

Time

Notes

投入

复习

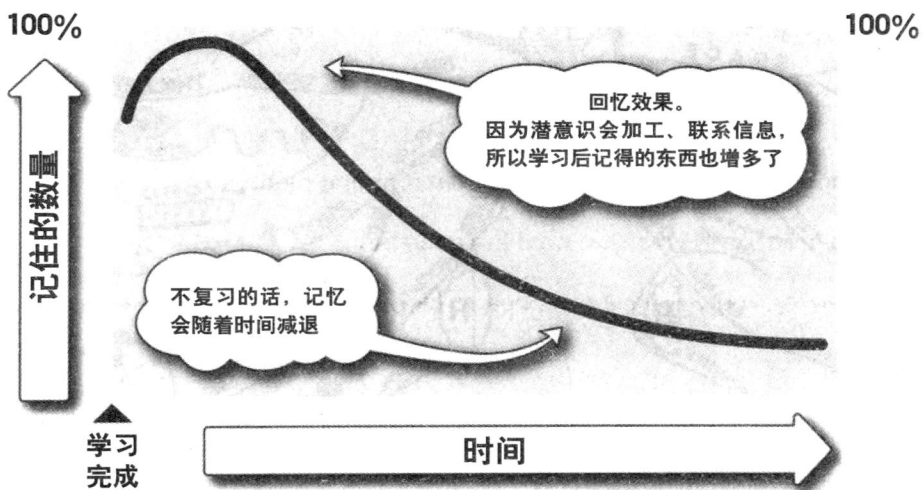

COMMITTING

REVIEW
WHY & HOW

- Once you have learned something, it is easier to keep that knowledge fresh than to start again

- Do not let what you have learned go to waste

- **Reviewing** embeds that knowledge in your long-term memory

- Repetition is not enough – **use a different learning method**
  - review mind maps by re-creating
  - then review only what you want to remember
  - key facts only
  - not everything you have read, heard, seen or done

Notes

投入

复习

为什么和怎么样

- 学到了某种知识后，记住它们比重新开始更容易

- 不要浪费了所学的内容

- **复习**能帮助你将所学知识变为长期记忆

- 仅仅重复是不够的——**要使用不同的学习方法**
——通过重建来复习思维导图
——只复习那些你想记住的信息
——仅仅是关键信息
——不是你读到的、听到的、看到的或是做过的所有内容

COMMITTING

REVIEW

WHEN

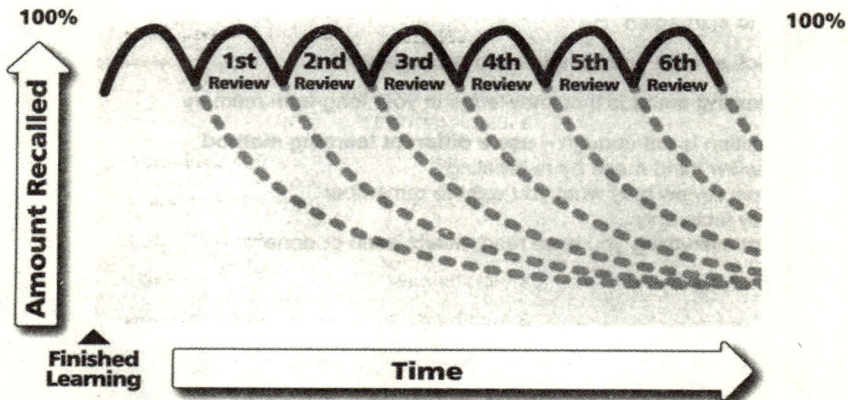

Notes

_____

_____

_____

_____

_____

投入

复习

何时

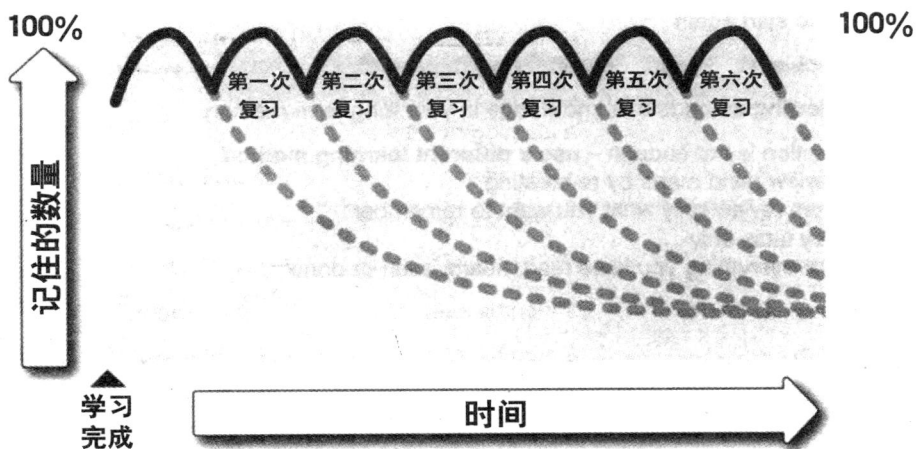

COMMITTING

REVIEW
WHEN

REVIEW	WHEN	HOW LONG
1st review	10–30 minutes after a learning event	For 5 minutes
2nd review	1 day after	For 5 minutes
3rd review	1 week after	For 5 minutes
4th review	1 month after	For 3 minutes
5th review	3 months after	For 3 minutes
6th review	6 months after	For 3 minutes

Stored in long-term memory

Notes

_____

_____

_____

_____

_____

投入

复习

何时

复习	何时	多久
第一次复习	学习之后 10–30 分钟	5 分钟
第二次复习	1 天后	5 分钟
第三次复习	1 周后	5 分钟
第四次复习	1 个月后	3 分钟
第五次复习	3 个月后	3 分钟
第六次复习	6 个月后	3 分钟
存储在长期记忆里		

COMMITTING

MENTORING

- A mentor is an individual skilled in the area you are learning
- They should be supportive and provide further information
- Watch them, talk to them, use their ideas and methods
- There should be a two way contract which is mutually beneficial to both parties – even if it is only buying lunch, while you pick their brains
- Return the favour to someone else by being a mentor yourself

Notes

_____

_____

_____

_____

投入

指导

- 导师是十分擅长于你学习的领域的人

- 他们应该很支持你，提供进一步的信息

- 观察他们，和他们交流，采用他们的想法和方法

- 应该签订一个互惠互利的双向合同——甚至只是请他们吃饭，你可以从他们身上学到东西

- 自己也可以成为一个导师并教导别人

REFLECTING

反 思

REFLECTING

TEST YOURSELF

Have you learned?

- Before testing yourself, set a standard and keep it
- Speed is not important – getting it right is
- Use, or create, mock exams
- Use mental rehearsal/visualisation
- Re-create mind maps from memory
- Teach others (your learning set) – this really proves if you know your stuff
- If you are learning to learn – learn something, put it to the test

Notes

反思

自我测试

你学会了吗？

• 在自我测试前，设立一个标准并遵守该标准

• 速度不重要——正确才是关键

• 使用、创造、模仿测试

• 在大脑里彩排、可视化

• 根据记忆重建思维导图

• 教会别人（你的学习小组）——这能真正证明你是否了解你的员工

• 如果你正在学习如何学习的话，那就学习一些东西，然后进行测试

REFLECTING

TEST YOURSELF

If you learn to drive, you get in a car.
If you learn to swim, you jump in the water. So:

- If you are learning how to mind map – mind map books, TV, documentaries, etc
- If you are learning how to write – put pen to paper
- If you are learning French – *parlez francais*
- If you are learning Chinese cookery – buy a wok and start using it
- If you are learning about computers – sit in front of one and use it
- If you are learning how to deliver speeches – stand up and talk
- If you are learning book keeping – get your calculator out
- If you are learning how to learn – learn something, use the techniques in this book

No child has learned to talk only by watching others and reading about it; sooner or later they open their mouth.

Notes

_____

_____

_____

_____

_____

反思

自我测试

如果你学开车的话，首先得进入车里。

如果你学游泳的话，首先得跳进水里。所以：

- 如果你要学习如何使用思维导图的话，就拿书本、电视、纪录片等来练手吧

- 如果你要学习如何写作的话，让笔在纸上动起来吧

- 如果你要学习法语的话，开始说法语吧（parlez francais）

- 如果你要学习中国烹饪的话，买个锅用起来吧

- 如果你要学习电脑的话，坐在电脑前多多练习吧

- 如果你要学习演讲的话，站起来开始说话吧

- 如果你要学习记账的话，把计算器拿出来吧

- 如果你要学习如何学习的话，就使用本书中的技巧学点东西吧

没有哪个孩子只看别人讲话或是阅读就能学会讲话的；他们迟早得开口说话。

REFLECTING

LEARNING SET

Test yourselves:
- Present your learning to the set
- Test the set
  - set tests
  - run quizzes
  - have question and answer sessions
- Compete against other learning sets

Ask yourselves:

What worked well?
What could we do better next time?

Points to consider:
- Contract
- Competition
- Support
- Mix of styles
- Openness
- Quality of work
- Roles
- Benefits

Notes

_____

_____

_____

_____

_____

反思

学习小组

自我测试：

- 把你的学习成果展示给小组成员
- 测试小组
    - ——设定测试
    - ——进行测试
    - ——有问答环节
- 和其他小组竞赛

需要考虑：

- 合同
- 竞争
- 支持
- 不同风格
- 开放性
- 工作质量
- 角色
- 好处

问你自己：

哪方面效果不错？
哪方面下次我们可以做得更好？

REFLECTING

IMPROVING

What worked well?

What could I do better next time?

If you ask these questions and act on the answers, you will develop your learning ability.

It is as important to understand and repeat what did work well as it is to improve on anything that did not.

Remember – you are responsible for your own learning.

Notes

_____

_____

_____

_____

_____

反思

提高

哪方面效果比较好？

哪方面我下次可以做得更好？

如果你问这些问题并且按答案做的话，你的学习能力会得到提高。

了解、重复去做效果好的方面和改进效果不好的方面一样重要。

记住——你要对自己的学习负责。

REFLECTING

REWARD

You should recognise and reward your successes.
- It encourages positive emotions about learning
- Ensures learning is fun, rewarding, enjoyable and worth doing again

Incentives should be given along the way, but, in particular, at the end of a learning event. The reward is not: having the knowledge, passing the exam, getting the qualification, achieving the promotion or the feeling that any of this gives you. Reward is:

- Eating out at a special restaurant
- Having a weekend break
- Going to the theatre
- Doing something unusual:
  - bungee jumping
  - driving a racing car
  - water ski-ing, etc
- Sharing your success with others

> **How will you reward yourself for learning how to learn?**

Notes

_____

_____

_____

_____

_____

反思

奖励

你应该认可并奖励自己的成功。

- 这能鼓励积极的学习情绪
- 确保学习很有趣、有回报、让人享受并且值得再次进行

学习过程中应该给予奖励，但学习之后更要奖励。奖励不是：收获知识、通过考试、获得资格、得到提升或是这些当中任何一个给你的感受。奖励是：

- 在一家有特色的餐馆吃饭
- 周末休息
- 去剧院
- 做一些不同的事：
    - ——蹦极
    - ——开赛车
    - ——滑水，等等
- 和别人分享你的成功

对于学习如何学习，你会如何奖励自己呢？

MEMORY TECHNIQUES

记忆技巧

MEMORY TECHNIQUES

METHODS

Principles	– Principles are easier to recall than individual examples, eg *i before e, except after c*, or *when sounded like a, as in neighbour or weigh*'
Rhyme	– Makes use of musical intelligence, eg *30 days hath September* ...
Acronym	– Forming a word from the first letter(s) of other words, eg:

H uron
O ntario
M ichigan   The great lakes
E rie
S uperior

Mnemonic	– Generic term for any memory aid, eg '**E**very **G**ood **B**oy **D**eserves **F**avour' **EGBDF**, the musical notes on the line of the stave
Storytelling	– Although it may be many years later, the moral of a story sticks with us, eg *The Tortoise and the Hare*.

Notes

_____

_____

_____

_____

_____

记忆技巧

方法

原则 ——原则比个例更容易记住，比如拼写单词时 i 通常在 e 前，除非 i 前出现了 c 或是听起来像 a 时，比如 neighbour 或 weigh。

押韵 ——发挥音乐智能，比如：30 days hath September…（9 月有 30 天）。

首字母缩略词 —— 一些单词的首字母构成的词，比如：

H uron　　休伦湖
O ntario　　安大略湖
M ichigan　密歇根湖　　　　五大湖
E rie　　　伊利湖
S uperior　苏必利尔湖

记忆术 ——任何记忆辅助的通称，比如"每个好男孩都值得喜欢（**E**VERY **G**OOD **B**OY **D**ESERVES **F**AVOR）"，**EGBDF** 即是五线谱上的音符。

讲故事 ——多年之后故事的寓意还会记在我们心里，比如龟兔赛跑。

MEMORY TECHNIQUES

NUMBERS

Numbers are traditionally hard to remember. They lack feeling, image, motion, humour and are, in comparison to a word, meaningless.

Use the following method to convert numbers to words and pictures, therefore making them easier to remember.

Number	Code	Remember
0	S, Z	first sound of the word zero
1	T, D	both t and d have one downstroke
2	N	n has two downstrokes
3	M	m has three downstrokes
4	R	final sound of the word 'four'
5	L	roman numeral for 50, make L with your hand (5 digits)
6	J, CH, SH soft G	j turned around is like the number 6
7	K, hard C, hard G	k formed from two 7s, one reversed
8	F, V	f and 8 both have two loops, one above the other
9	P, B	p reversed is 9

Notes

記憶技巧

数字

数字一般很难记。它们没有感觉、图像、动作、幽默，而且不像单词，它们是没有意义的。

使用下面的方法将数字转化成单词、图片，这样就容易记忆了。

数字	代码	记住
0	S，Z	单词 zero 的第一个音节
1	T，D	t 和 d 都有一竖
2	N	n 有两竖
3	M	m 有三竖
4	R	单词 four 的最后一个音节
5	L	罗马数字 50，用你的手做一个 L (5 个手指)
6	J，CH，SH 线条柔和的 G	j 转过来就像数字 6
7	K，棱角分明的 C，棱角分明的 G	k 由两个 7 组成，其中一个是倒过来的
8	F，V	f 和 8 都有两个圈，一个在另一个上面
9	P，B	p 反过来就是 9

MEMORY TECHNIQUES

NUMBERS IN PRACTICE

This system can be used to remember any sequence of numbers, eg:

123	=	DNM	=	**Denim**	
921210	=	PNDNTS	=	**Pound notes**	

(number) → (word) → (picture) →

Vowels and the letter W, H and Y (WHY) have no meaning under this system and are used to complete words.

What about the following?

(number) → (word) → (picture) →

54226 = ? ? ? ? ? = ?

Answer at bottom of page

Practise the system regularly, break numbers down into words for speed.
Based on the work of Stanislaus Mink Von Wennsshein 1648 and Dr Richard Grey 1730

54226 = L R N N G = Learning

Notes

_____

_____

_____

_____

_____

记忆技巧

数字练习

这个系统可以用来记住任何数字组合，比如：

123 = DNM = **Denim**
921210 = PNDNTS = **Pound notes**

数字 > 单词 > 图像 >

元音和字母 W、H、Y（WHY）在这个系统下是没有意义的。它们是用来完成单词的。

下面的呢？

数字 > 单词 > 图像 >
54226 = ? ? ? ? ? = ?　　答案见本页底边

定期练习该系统，迅速把数字转化成单词。

（基于坦尼斯劳斯·明克·冯·文斯欣 1648 年和理查德·格瑞 1730 年的作品。）

NUMBERS

The number system covered is worth learning; why not try the following method too, eg:

Pi = 0.318310 .....   0. 3 1 8 3 10
                              Can I remember the reciprocal

The letters in each word total the number you want to remember.

What about our earlier number 5 4 2 2 6 ? Try to come up with a memorable phrase.

Suggestion at bottom of page.

Learn More is my number

Notes

_____

_____

_____

_____

_____

数字

前面介绍的数字系统很值得学习；为什么不也试一试下面的方法呢，比如：

Pi = 0.318310 .....

0. 3 1 8 3 10
Can I remember the reciprocal
（我能记住倒数吗？）

每个单词的字母数都等于你想要记住的那个数字。

之前的数字 54226 呢？看看能不能找到一个容易记住的短语？本页底边有参考版本。

MEMORY TECHNIQUES

DATES

Try using the system covered earlier, on page 216.

Wall Street Crash   1929   2 = N, 9 = P

N a P = Picture yourself driving a car, having a nap and crashing into a wall.

Chamberlain declares war on Germany   3/9/1939   3 = M, 9 = D

M a D M a D =   Picture a mad and angry Chamberlain fighting a mad and angry Hitler.

And/or try a time line:

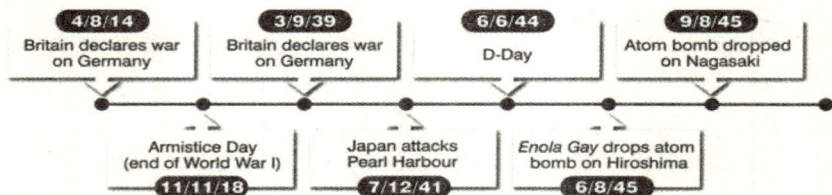

4/8/14	3/9/39	6/6/44	9/8/45
Britain declares war on Germany	Britain declares war on Germany	D-Day	Atom bomb dropped on Nagasaki

Armistice Day (end of World War I)	Japan attacks Pearl Harbour	*Enola Gay* drops atom bomb on Hiroshima
11/11/18	7/12/41	6/8/45

Notes

_____

_____

_____

_____

_____

记忆技巧

日期

试试使用 217 页提到的系统。

华尔街崩盘　　1929　2 = N，9 = P

N a P = 想象自己开着车，打了个盹就撞到墙上了

张伯伦对德宣战　　3/9/1939　3 = M，9 = D

M a D　M a D = 想象一下疯狂且愤怒的张伯伦对战疯狂且愤怒的希特勒。

并且（或者）试试时间轴：

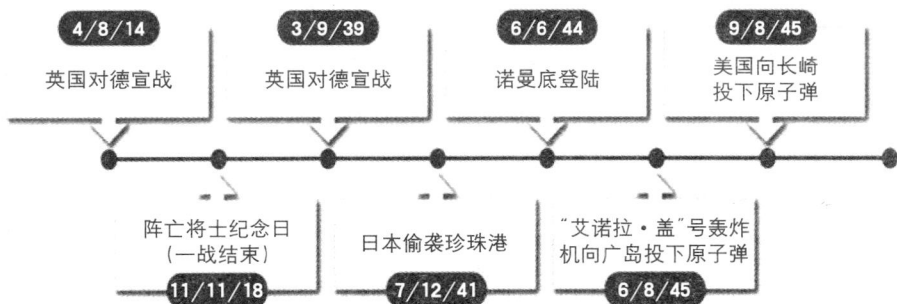

PEG SYSTEMS

This is a method used for remembering lists and sequences. You use a memorised sequence of hooks, on to which you link new information. (For effective links, see **Linking**, page 166.) Make your peg system personal by creating your own words and images. Personal ideas are easier to recall. (The number system below could be used as a peg system, giving you thousands of pegs on to which you can link new information.)

Number System

1	=	D		=	Day
2	=	N		=	Noah
3	=	M		=	May
4	=	R		=	Ray
5	=	L		=	Lay
6	=	J (ch, sh, soft g)		=	Jay
7	=	K		=	Key
8	=	F (l, v)		=	Fee
9	=	B (l, p)		=	Bay
10	=	DZ		=	Daze

Number Rhyme

1	=	Gun
2	=	Chew
3	=	Tree
4	=	Door
5	=	Hive
6	=	Bricks
7	=	Heaven
8	=	Gate
9	=	Wine
10	=	Hen

Notes

_____

_____

_____

_____

_____

记忆技巧

挂钩记忆系统

这是个用来记忆列表和序列的方法。使用一些你已经记住的挂钩顺序，你把新信息联系在它们上面。（为获得有效联系，参见167页"**联系**"部分。）用自己的话和图像形成自己的专属挂钩记忆系统。自己的想法更容易记住。（下面的数字系统可以被用来当做挂钩记忆系统，数以千计的挂钩可以供你把新信息联系在它们上面）

数字系统			
1	=	D	= Day
2	=	N	= Noah
3	=	M	= May
4	=	R	= Ray
5	=	L	= Lay
6	=	J(ch, sh, soft g)	= Jay
7	=	K	= Key
8	=	F(l, v)	= Fee
9	=	B(l, p)	= Bay
10	=	DZ	= Daze

数字押韵	
1	= Gun
2	= Chew
3	= Tree
4	= Door
5	= Hive
6	= Bricks
7	= Heaven
8	= Gate
9	= Wine
10	= Hen

MEMORY TECHNIQUES

PEG SYSTEMS
NUMBER SHAPE

1 = Pen

2 = Swan

3 = Hills

4 = Boat

5 = Hook

6 = Yo-Yo

7 = Boomerang

8 = Egg-timer

9 = Flag

10 = Bat & ball

 *Notes*

记忆技巧

挂钩记忆系统

数字形状

1 ＝ 笔

6 ＝ 溜溜球

2 ＝ 天鹅

7 ＝ 飞去来器

3 ＝ 山

8 ＝ 煮蛋计时器

4 ＝ 船

9 ＝ 旗子

5 ＝ 挂钩

10 ＝ 球拍 & 球

MEMORY TECHNIQUES

PEG SYSTEMS

ALPHABET SYSTEM

The peg word must start with the sound of the letter, eg:
A = **Ace** not **Apple**, C - **Sea** not **Cat**.

A	=	Ace	J	=	Jay	S	=	Eskimo
B	=	Bee	K	=	Cake	T	=	Tea
C	=	Sea	L	=	Elbow	U	=	Yew
D	=	Deed	M	=	Empire	V	=	Venus
E	=	Easel	N	=	Enema	W	=	WC
F	=	Effluent	O	=	Obese	X	=	X-ray
G	=	Gee Gee	P	=	Pea	Y	=	Y-fronts
H	=	H-Bomb	Q	=	Queue	Z	=	Z car
I	=	Eye	R	=	Arm			

Notes

记忆技巧

挂钩记忆系统

字母表系统

挂钩单词的第一个音节必须和那个字母的发音相同，比如：
A = **A**ce（纸牌A）而不是 **A**pple（苹果），C— **S**ea（大海）而不是 **C**at（猫）。

A = Ace	J = Jay	S = Eskimo
B = Bee	K = Cake	T = Tea
C = Sea	L = Elbow	U = Yew
D = Deed	M = Empire	V = Venus
E = Easel	N = Enema	W = WC
F = Effluent	O = Obese	X = X—ray
G = Gee Gee	P = Pea	Y = Y—fronts
H = H—Bomb	Q = Queue	Z = Z car
I = Eye	R = Arm	

MEMORY TECHNIQUES

PEG SYSTEMS

Days of the Week

Sunday	–	sun
Monday	–	money
Tuesday	–	chew
Wednesday	–	wedding
Thursday	–	thirsty
Friday	–	fry
Saturday	–	saturn

Use your own *personal* images – more memorable.

Months of the year

January	–	New Year
February	–	Brewery
March	–	Marching
April	–	Ape
May	–	Maypole
June	–	Bride
July	–	Jewel
August	–	Gust
September	–	Sceptre
October	–	Octopus
November	–	Fireworks
December	–	Christmas

Notes

记忆技巧

挂钩记忆系统

一周的每一天

Sunday （周日） ——	sun （太阳）
Monday （周一） ——	money （金钱）
Tuesday （周二） ——	chew （咀嚼）
Wednesday（周三） ——	wedding（婚礼）
Thursday （周四） ——	thirsty （口渴）
Friday （周五） ——	fry （油煎）
Saturday （周六 ） ——	Saturn （土星）

使用你自己的图像，这样更容易记住。

一年的每一月

January （一月） ——	New Year （新年）
February （二月） ——	Brewery （啤酒厂）
March （三月） ——	Marching （前进）
April （四月） ——	Ape （类人猿）
May （五月） ——	Maypole （五朔节花柱）
June （六月） ——	Bride （新娘）
July （七月） ——	Jewel （珠宝）
August （八月） ——	Gust （狂风）
September （九月） ——	Sceptre （权杖）
October （十月） ——	Octopus （章鱼）
November （十一月） ——	Fireworks （烟花）
December （十二月） ——	Christmas （圣诞）

BLOCKS TO LEARNING

学习障碍

BLOCKS TO LEARNING

OVERCOMING BLOCKS TO LEARNING

Psychological: **Wrong state of mind, negative attitude to learning, fear**
Use relaxation techniques to prepare for learning and exercise regularly
Have a clear focus on why you are learning
Use positive affirmations and visualisation to reinforce success
Reward yourself, make learning fun
Use your learning set or mentor to support your fears and praise your success

Physiological: **Poor environment, distractions, too comfortable and relaxed**
Prepare your environment for learning
Avoid distractions, such as noise, visual distractions and comfortable armchairs

Learning style: **Not knowing how you learn best**
Find your strengths and use them to your advantage

Notes

学习障碍

克服学习障碍

心理上：错误的心态，消极的学习态度，恐惧

使用放松技巧为学习做准备，经常锻炼

清楚地知道自己为什么学习

采用积极肯定和可视化来加强成功

奖励自己，让学习变得有趣

求助于学习小组或导师消除你的恐惧，赞扬你的成功

生理上：不良环境，有干扰，过于舒服和放松

营造良好的学习环境

免除干扰，比如噪音、视觉干扰、舒服的扶手椅

学习方式：不知道哪种方式学习效果最佳

发现自己的优点并发挥它们的作用

OVERCOMING BLOCKS TO LEARNING

Time:	**Not having the time, learning solidly for hours, burning the midnight oil – especially prior to an exam** Plan out your learning (use a learning plan) Prior to an exam, relax – don't cram. With a learning plan all your learning will have been completed
Subject:	**Lack of interest, lack of understanding** Have a clear focus on why you are learning Reward yourself Read simple introductory texts at first Prepare your questions (the six W's) and get involved
Experience:	**Previous bad experiences of learning** All of the above may have caused this experience Is it really as bad as you perceive or have you created it? You cannot change the past, but now is the time to move on

Notes

学习障碍

克服学习障碍

时间 ：没有时间，长时间苦读，挑灯夜战——尤其是考试前
规划好学习（制定学习计划）
考前尽量放松，不要填鸭似地学习。制定学习计划的话，所有的学习任务都会完成。

课题 ：没有兴趣，理解不了
清楚地知道自己为什么学习
奖励自己
先阅读简单的介绍性文字
准备问题（六个 W），积极参与

经历 ：之前不理想的学习经历
上面提到的内容都有可能引起这种经历
它真像你想的那么糟吗？还是一切都是你想象出来的？
你无法改变过去，能做的就是把握现在

MASTER MIND MAP – LEARNING
REVIEW
MIND MAP
TRICKS
RECENCY
PRIMACY
LINKING
OUTSTANDINGNESS
STUDY
AIDS
SENSORY
SHORT
TYPES
LONG
STAGES
MAY
REGISTRATION
INTELLIGENCES
RETENTION
RETRIEVAL
STYLE
V.A.K.
6 x W
MEMORY
NEWS PAPER
POWER READING
LEARNING
SET
COMMITTING
REWARD
IMPROVE
TEST
REFLECTING
LEARNER'S POCKETBOOK

Notes

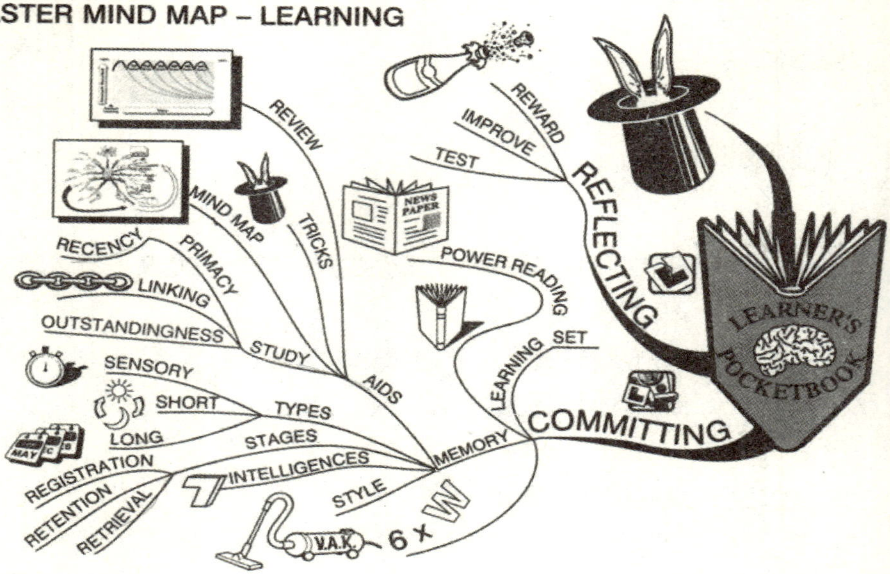

掌握思维导图——学习

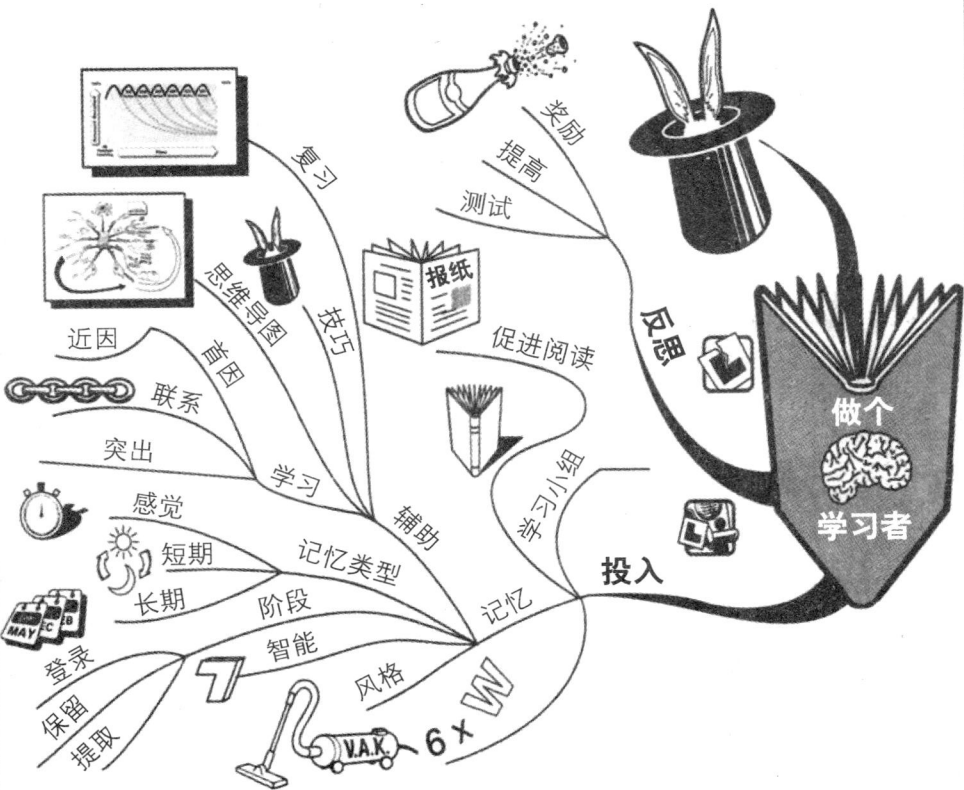

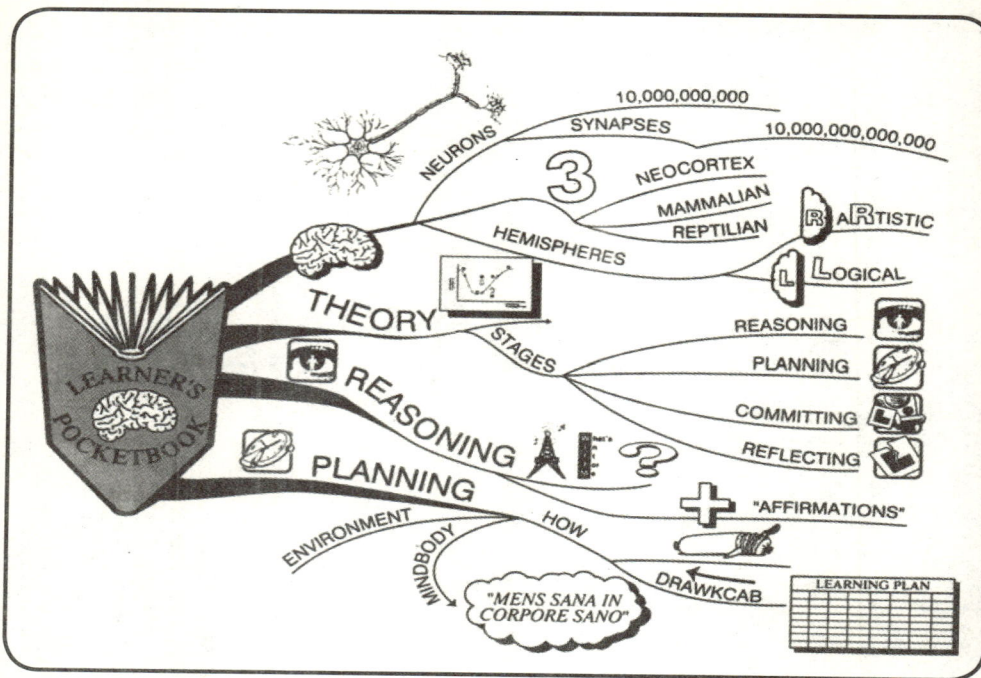

Notes

_____

_____

_____

_____

_____

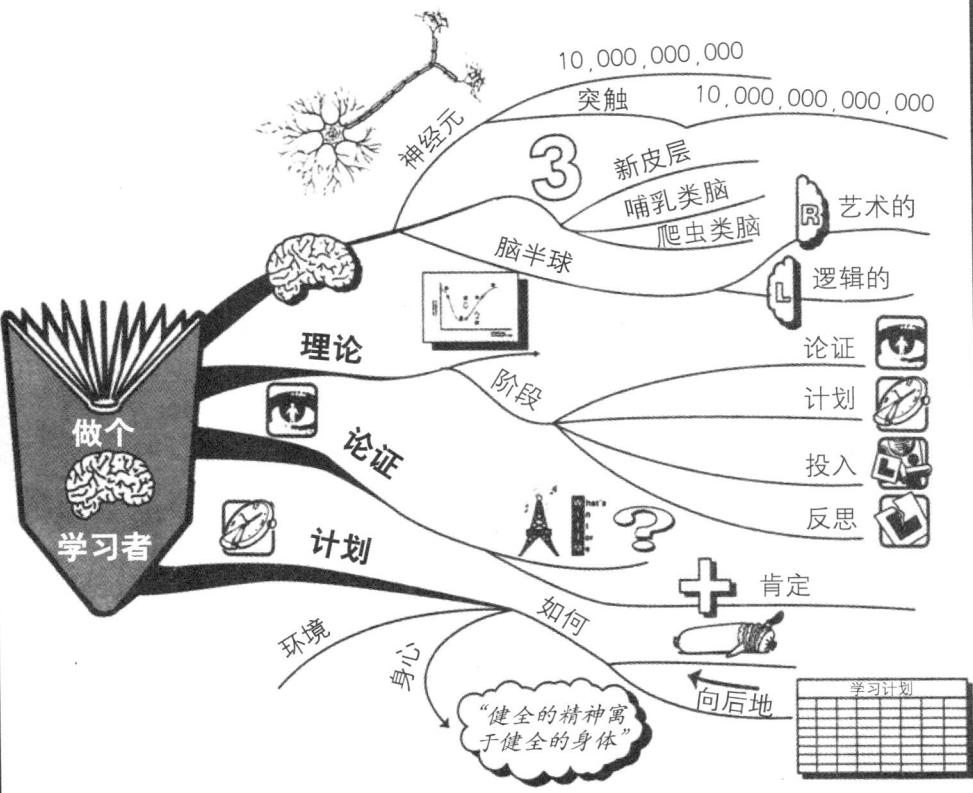

参考文献

Make the Most of your Mind
Tony Buzan, Pan (1998)

Use your Memory
Tony Buzan, BBC Books (2003)

The Learning Revolution
Gordon Dryden & Dr Jeannette Vos
Network Educational Press (2001)

Total Recall
J Minninger PhD
MJF Books (1997)

Get Ahead
Vanda North & Tony Buzan

Superlearning
Sheila Ostander & Lynn Schroeder
Souvenir Press (1996)

Rapid Reading
Kathryn Redway
Contemporary Books (1991)

Accelerated Learning
Colin Rose
Accelerated Learning Systems (1985)

Accelerate Your Learning
Colin Rose & Louise Croll
Accelerated Learning Systems (1992)

The Brain Book
Peter Russell, Taylor & Francis (1980)

How to Boost your Brain Power
Roger B Yepsen, Jnr
Little, Brown & Co. (2000)

Multiple Intelligences: The Theory In Practice
Howard Gardner, Basic Books (1993)

The Accelerated Learning Pocketbook
Brin Best, Teachers' Pocketbooks (2003)

Head First
Tony Buzan. Harper Collins (2000)

The Fragrant Mind
Valerie Ann Worwood, Bantam (1997)

关于作者

保罗·海顿，英国销售和营销管理学院研究员，地中海基础物理学协会成员，获得个人理财学位证书

保罗经营着自己的培训与咨询公司，他的客户包括毕马威国际会计公司、苏格兰银行、IBM、保诚和业通。作为一名培训顾问，他致力于开发广泛的技能和知识去帮助个人和公司，使他们的潜能得到最大发挥。

在经营自己的公司之前，他在联合邓巴负责培养总部人员，而后负责培养销售人员。保罗出过很多培训手册，是《个人成功》的作者和《财务顾问的指导》的作者之一。

联系方式

如果你想就他的观点和方法咨询保罗·海顿，你可以通过以下途径与他取得联系：邮寄地址 The Hayden Partnership，P O Box 965，Swindon，Wiltshire SN5 5YS。固定电话 01793 772844；传真 01793 772844；移动电话 07768 012316；邮箱 paul@haydenpartnership.com；网址 www.haydenpartnership.com。

英汉对照管理丛书

英汉对照管理袖珍手册